The Spider
And Other Tales

Carl Ewald

Alpha Editions

This edition published in 2024

ISBN : 9789361471100

Design and Setting By
Alpha Editions
www.alphaedis.com
Email - info@alphaedis.com

As per information held with us this book is in Public Domain.
This book is a reproduction of an important historical work. Alpha Editions uses the best technology to reproduce historical work in the same manner it was first published to preserve its original nature. Any marks or number seen are left intentionally to preserve its true form.

THE SPIDER

1

THE hedge had once been full of trees and bushes, but they were cut down and nothing now shot up from their stubs but long, thin twigs.

In between the stubs grew goat's-foot and fool's-parsley and more weeds of the same kind, which all look like one another and are called wild chervil by people who know no better.

Their branches were almost as long as those of the bushes. And they were as pretentious as though they really were bushes and as though they did not wither in the autumn and have to start all over again with a little seed, just like some silly daisy or pansy. They strutted and swaggered, they rustled in the wind, they snapped, they lost their leaves and got new ones, exactly as if their time were their own. If any one asked them what they really were, they pretended not to hear, or turned it off as a jest, or refused pointblank to answer.

And then they had beautiful white flowers, which they lifted high in the air, like parasols, whereas the real branches, that grew on the stubs, never got to look like anything but overgrown children and could put forth neither flowers nor fruit.

2

"Why, here's quite a wood!" said the mouse, one evening, sitting under the foliage and peeping up with her bright eyes.

"We are the wood," said the goat's-foot.

"Pray take a look round," said the parsley. "If you like us, build your nest in us. All that we can offer you is at your service."

"Don't believe them," said the real bushes. "They only make a show while summer lasts. When autumn comes, they are gone without leaving a trace behind them."

"I don't know anything about autumn," said the parsley.

"I don't believe in autumn," said the goat's-foot. "It's a cock-and-bull story with which they take in the baby bushes."

"Autumn exists all right," said the mouse. "And after that comes winter. Then the thing is to have one's larder full. It's well I thought of it. I think I will dig myself a little hole between the stones and begin laying up."

"Let him burrow in the ground that pleases," said the parsley.

"We have loftier aims," said the goat's-foot.

Then they stood a bit and said nothing. And then the parsley sighed and said what they were both thinking.

"If only a bird would come and build her nest in us!"

"We would shade it and rock it and take such care of it that the real bushes would die of envy," said the goat's-foot.

"Won't you have me?" asked a voice.

A queer, gray individual came walking up the hedge.

"Who are you?" asked the parsley.

"I am the spider," said the individual.

"Can you fly?" asked the goat's-foot.

"I can do a little of everything, if need be."

"Do you eat flies?" asked the parsley.

"All day long."

"Do you lay eggs?" asked the goat's-foot. "For, of course, you're a woman?"

"Yes—thank goodness!" said the spider.

"Then you're the bird for us," said the parsley.

"You're heartily welcome," said the goat's-foot. "You look pretty light, so you won't break our branches. Be sure and begin to build as soon as you please. You'll find plenty of materials in the hedge."

"It doesn't matter in the least if you nip off a leaf here and there," said the parsley.

"Thanks, I carry my own materials with me," said the spider.

"I don't see any luggage," said the goat's-foot.

"Perhaps your husband's bringing it?" asked the parsley.

"I have no husband, thank goodness!" said the spider.

"Poor thing!" said the mouse, who sat listening. "That must be awfully sad for you."

"Ah, there's the usual feminine balderdash!" said the spider. "That's what makes us women such ridiculous and contemptible creatures. It's always 'my husband' here and 'my husband' there. I should like to know what use a husband is to one, when all's said. He's nothing but a nuisance and a worry. If ever I take another, he sha'n't live with me, whatever happens."

"How you talk!" said the mouse. "I can't think of anything more dismal than if my husband were to live away from me. And I should like to know how I should manage with the children, if he didn't help me, the dear soul!"

"Children!" replied the spider. "Fiddle-de-dee! I don't see the use of all that coddling. Lay your eggs in a sensible place and then leave them alone."

"She doesn't talk like a bird," said the parsley, doubtfully.

"I too am beginning to be uneasy about her," said the goat's-foot.

"You can call me what you like," said the spider. "In any case, I don't associate with the other birds. If there are too many of them here, I won't even stay."

"Lord preserve us!" said the parsley, who began to fear lest she should go away. "There are hardly ever any here."

"They flew into the wood when the trees were cut down," said the goat's-foot.

"Yes, it's dull here," said the long twigs on the stubs. "One never hears a note."

"It's all right here," said the spider. "As long as the flies buzz, I'm content."

"Here we are!" said the goat's-foot and the parsley, straightening themselves.

The spider crawled about and looked around her and the mouse kept on following her with her eyes:

"I beg your pardon," said she. "But why do you build a nest when you leave your eggs to shift for themselves?"

"Listen to me, Mousie," said the spider. "You may as well look upon me from the start as an independent woman. I think only of myself and my belongings and I look after myself. If I ever condescend to take a husband, the milksop will have to look after himself."

"Lord, how you speak of him!" said the mouse. "My husband is bigger and stronger than I am."

"I have never met him," replied the spider, carelessly. "The men in my family are scarce a quarter as large as I am. Wretched creatures, not worth a fly. I should be ashamed to share my flat with a customer like one of those. But now I'm going to build."

"You had better wait till it's light," said the parsley.

"What will you build with?" asked the goat's-foot.

"I like the dark, as it happens," said the spider. "And I carry my own building-materials."

Then she scrambled to the top of the goat's-foot and looked round the landscape.

"You must have good eyes to see at night," said the mouse. "Mine are not bad, but still I shouldn't care to build a nest by this light."

"As for eyes, I have eight," said the spider. "And they see what they have to. I have also eight legs, I may as well tell you, and you needn't be struck with amazement on that account. Taken all round, I am a woman who knows how to help herself in an emergency. There's no coddling here and no nonsense."

Now she pressed her abdomen against the branch of the goat's-foot on which she was sitting and then took a header into the air.

"She'll break her neck!" cried the mouse, terrified.

"I haven't got a neck," said the spider, from down below. "And, if I had, I wouldn't break it. You go home to your dear husband and fondle him. When you come back in the morning, you shall see what a capable woman can do who doesn't waste her time on love and emotions."

The mouse went away, because she had other things to see to and also because the spider's words hurt her. But the goat's-foot and the fool's-parsley were obliged to remain where they were and so were the long twigs on the stubs. And the spider behaved in such a curious manner that none of them closed an eye all night for looking at her.

The fact is, she did nothing but take headers into the air. She jumped first from one branch and then from another, then crawled up again and jumped once more. And, although she had no wings, as any one could see, she let herself down quite slowly to the ground or to another branch, never missed her jump and did not come to the least harm. To and fro, up and down she went, the whole night long.

"It *is* a bird," said the parsley, delightedly.

"Of course," said the goat's-foot. "What else could it be?"

But the twigs on the stubs bobbed at one another mockingly:

"She's never been a bird in her life," they said. "Can she sing? Have you heard as much as a chirp from her?"

The goat's-foot and the parsley looked at each other doubtfully. And, when the spider sat still, for a moment, catching her breath, the parsley ventured upon a question:

"Can you sing?"

"Pshaw!" replied the spider. "Do you think I go in for that sort of twaddle? What is there to sing about? Life is nothing but toil and drudgery and, if a lone woman is to hold her own, she must turn to and set to work."

"Birds sing," said the goat's-foot.

"They sing because they are in love," said the spider. "I am not in love."

"Wait till the right man comes along," said the parsley.

"If he does, he'd better look out," said the spider.

Then she took another header; and so she went on.

3

But, when the day began to break, the goat's-foot and the parsley were near snapping with surprise.

The spider was hanging in the air between their branches. She had drawn her legs up under her, bundled herself together and was sleeping like a top.

"Is she on you?" asked the goat's-foot.

"No," replied the parsley. "Is she on you?"

"No," said the goat's-foot.

"She's not on us either," said the twigs.

"It *is* a bird," said the parsley and the goat's-foot, enraptured.

"A bird doesn't hang in the middle of the air, sleeping," said the twigs.

"It's an elf," said the mouse, who came up at that moment. "Just wait till it's quite light: then perhaps we shall see."

And, when the sun rose, they saw.

In between the branches of the goat's-foot and the fool's-parsley were stretched a number of very fine threads, which crossed one another and shone in the sun so that it was a delight to see. Other threads ran across them in circles, one outside the other.

"Ah!" said the mouse. "Now I understand. She was sitting in the middle of that. But where has she gone to now?"

"Here I am," said the spider, from under a leaf. "I can't stand the bright sunlight. What do you think of my work? But I haven't finished yet."

"Pish!" said the mouse. "Frankly speaking, I think it's a funny sort of nest you've made."

"Nest, nest, nest!" said the spider. "It's you who've been talking of a nest, not I. You keep on taking it for granted that I am a silly, effeminate woman like yourself and the others. What use is a nest to me? I'm all right here under this leaf. It's shady here and good enough for me. The threads are my web. I catch flies in it. I wonder, shall we have a little rain? Then I can set to again and finish my work."

Presently, the sun disappeared behind the clouds. A mild and gentle rain fell and when it stopped the spider came out and stretched her eight legs contentedly in the moist air.

And then she set to work.

They all saw how she pulled a multitude of very fine threads at a time from her abdomen. Then she began to unravel them with combs which she had at the ends of her legs, twisted them together into one thick thread and hung it beside the others where she thought that the opening was too large or the net not strong enough. All the threads were greasy and sticky, so that the flies would have to hang fast in them. Later in the day, the web was ready; and they all admired it because it was so pretty.

"Now I'm settled," said the spider.

At that moment came a starling and sat on the top of one of the long twigs:

"Is there nothing to eat here?" he asked. "A few grubs? A spider or so?"

The goat's-foot and the parsley said nothing: they almost withered with fright at the idea of losing their lodger. The mouse made off, for safety's sake, but the twigs on the stubs cried with one breath that a nice fat spider had just come and had spun her web in the night.

"I can see none," said the starling and flew away.

But the spider, quick as lightning, had let herself down to the ground by a long thread and lay there as still as if she were dead. Now she crept up again and sat in the middle of her web with all her eight legs outstretched.

"That was a near thing," she said. "Now my turn's coming."

Up came a smart little fly, who didn't see the web but flew in and got caught, poor fellow.

"That's an earnest," said the spider.

She bit the fly with her mandibles, which were filled with poison, so that he died at once. Then she ate him. And she did the same with the next three that came into the web. After that, she could eat no more. She let a good many little insects, that had the misfortune to get caught, hang and sprawl, without stirring a limb. When a good fat fly came along, she bit him dead, spun a little web round him and hung him up:

"He may come in handy one day, when I run short," she said.

"Very sensible," said the mouse. "That's really the first thing you've said that I can agree with. But, otherwise, I am bound to say I don't care for your ways. They're far too sly for me. And then you use poison, like the adder. That, I think, is mean."

"You think so, do you?" said the spider, with a sneer. "Is it any worse than what you others do? I suppose you blow a trumpet when you sneak out after your prey; eh, you pious little mouse?"

"Indeed I could, if I had a trumpet," said the mouse. "Thank goodness, I am not a robber and murderer like yourself. I gather nuts and acorns and anything else that comes to hand and I have never hurt a soul."

"No, you're a dear little woman of the old-fashioned sort," said the spider, "You take other people's leavings and are quite happy. Then you go home and let your husband and children pet and fondle you. I'm not built that way, let me tell you. I don't care for caresses, but I have an appetite. I want meat: nice, juicy fly-meat; and lots of it. I ask nothing of anybody, but get myself what I want. If things go well, I have all the honour and pleasure myself; if they go badly, I don't go crying to anybody. It would be a good thing if there were more women like me."

"You're so rough," said the mouse.

"Fiddlesticks!" replied the spider. "It's all one. I'm no worse than most people. Take the goat's-foot and the parsley: they fight for the butterflies and bees and steal each other's light and air as much as they can."

"Very true," said the parsley.

"An exceedingly sensible woman," said the goat's-foot.

"That's such an ugly name of yours," said the mouse.

"Can't help that," said the spider. "Some people call me venom-head,[1] because of those few drops of poison I carry in my mandibles. They're so immensely upset about the poor flies I catch; and they kill a fly themselves if he only settles on their nose. It's six of one and half a dozen of the other. Nothing but sentimental affectation. Besides, I have no objection to changing my name. You can call me *spinner*, if you prefer. That's a word which a dainty little lady like you can pronounce without fainting; and it suits me, because there's not an animal in the world that spins as beautifully as I do."

"That's all very likely," said the mouse, shaking her head. "But what you do is ugly and you yourself are so hideous that there's no excusing you."

"Is that it?" asked the spider and laughed. "Look here, little Mrs. Mouse: I'm rationally dressed. My homely gray clothes suit my work and don't attract unnecessary attention. Thank goodness, I don't have to dress up like the others, who deck themselves out to obtain love and happiness and who strut and swagger in a way that a sensible person would be ashamed of. But, of course, the ninnies despise me for my plain frocks. Let them! What do I care for ninnies? And, if they come into my meshes, I'll eat them."

The mouse shook her head and went away. The parsley and the goat's-foot muttered softly to each other. The spider hung in her net, stretched her legs and digested her food.

When the sun came out, she crept under her leaf and then the mouse came back and peeped up:

"Is she asleep?" she asked.

"I think so," said the parsley. "And you had better not wake her with your chattering."

"She's our bird, once and for all," said the goat's-foot. "Though she may behave differently from other birds, she has done us the honour and shown us the confidence to build in us and therefore we ask that she may be respected."

"A nice sort of bird!" said the twigs, with a sneer.

"In any case, she's better than nothing," said the parsley.

"Such louts as you had better hold your tongues," said the goat's-foot. "No one builds in you, at any rate."

"She's not a bird," said the mouse. "But that's no reason why she shouldn't be very good. Now *I* think that she's a poor, unhappy old maid, who has fallen out with existence. Perhaps her sweetheart jilted her; that leaves a wound. My first husband ran away with a white mouse, just after my children were born. So I speak from experience."

"That's possible," said the parsley, thoughtfully. "But what can one do in a case like that?"

"We must try and make her happy," said the mouse. "If she goes on leading this lonely life, she will grow more bitter every day and at last all gentler feelings will be stifled in her. If we could only find a husband for her!"

"Yes, if we only could!" said the parsley.

"Then perhaps she would build a real nest, with little eggs in it," said the goat's-foot.

"Perhaps she would sing to her young," said the parsley.

"That would at once entitle us to rank with the bushes," said the goat's-foot.

"What are you talking about?" asked the spider, putting out her head from under the leaf.

"We're talking about you," said the mouse. "We were saying that you really ought to get married. It's not good, in the long run, for a woman to live alone. It makes her queer and sour. If you only knew how delightful it is to see one's dear little young and feed them and educate them!"

"Stuff!" said the spider.

"It's the provision of nature," said the mouse. "And I will do what I can for you, no matter what you say. I see a heap of spiders daily on my way along the hedge. They are certainly much smaller than you, but nice fellows, for all that. Perhaps I may meet a big one, too. Then I shall tell him that there's a charming young lady over here, longing for a sweetheart."

"Then you'll be telling an awful lie," said the spider. "And you needn't look for one who is bigger than I, for our men are all miserable under-sized vermin. I tell you, no one looks upon them as worth a straw. It's long been understood among us that it's only the women that are good for anything."

"Well, I'm going," said the mouse. "I shall find the right man yet. And I feel sure that you'll be much more amiable when you're in love."

"Run away, Mousie," said the spider. "The man who can please me isn't born yet. But you have nothing in your head but love and nonsense."

She killed a fly, spun a web round him and hung him up and then hid under the leaf. The mouse went away, the parsley and the goat's-foot put their heads together and talked of the future.

4

The next morning, a really nice gentleman-spider was sitting on the parsley, but a good way off from the snappish young lady.

He had brushed his clothes and spun a couple of fine threads to show what he could do. He bent and stretched his legs for her to see that he was well-shaped. Seven of his eyes beamed with love, while the eighth took care that she didn't eat him:

"Allow me, miss, to offer you my hand and heart," said he.

"He's a fair-spoken man," said the parsley.

"A charming man," said the goat's-foot.

"It was I that sent him here," said the mouse.

"Idiot!" said the damsel.

But the spider did not throw up the game so easily. He gracefully bowed his thorax, set two of his eyes to watch that nothing happened to him and looked doubly enamoured with the other six:

"Do not think that I mean to be a burden to you," he said. "I have my own web a little way down the hedge and I can easily catch the few flies I require. I have even got five real fat ones hanging and spun up, which I shall esteem it an honour to offer you to-morrow, so that you may see that it is love alone that urges me to propose to you."

"Is that you talking your nonsense?" said the damsel. "What the blazes should I do with such a silly man?"

"Dear me!" he said—and now there was only one eye in love, so fierce was her air—"If my courtship seems inopportune to you, I will retire at once and wait till another time...."

"I rather think that's the wisest thing you could do," said she. "Clear out, this minute, or I'll...."

He slid down a thread in no time and she after him. But he escaped and, a little later, she was sitting in her web again, looking sourer than ever.

"What a woman!" said the mouse.

"Yes, just so!" said the spider.

"It doesn't do to take the first that comes," said the parsley.

"It's only that he wasn't the right one," said the goat's-foot.

But the unfortunate suitor went round the hedge telling the other spiders about the charming and remarkable lady whose web hung between the parsley and the goat's-foot.

"She is *so* big," he said, spreading his legs as wide as he could. "I have never seen any one so pretty in my life. But she's as proud as a peacock. I shall certainly die of grief at her refusal. In any case, one thing is sure, that I shall never marry."

They listened to him wide-eyed and made him tell them again. It was not long before the story of the proud and beautiful spider-princess went the round of the hedge. As soon as the men had finished their day's work, they came together and sat and talked about her. Each of them had his own observations to make, but gradually they were all so excited with love that they thought they simply could not live unless they won the fair one.

One after the other, they set out a-wooing and they all fared badly.

The first was a dashing fellow, who had chaffed the unfortunate suitor mercilessly for promising her the five flies which he had got spun up at home in his web:

"Women don't care a hang for promises," he said. "They like their presents down, then and there. You just watch me."

He came dragging a splendid blue-bottle along and laid it without a word at the damsel's feet.

"Do you think I would allow a man to support me?" she said.

Before he could look round, she had caught him and eaten him up. She scornfully let the fly be, but, later in the afternoon, when she thought no one saw her, she came down notwithstanding and ate it.

And the wooers that came after fared not a whit better.

She ate six of them in the middle of their speech and two had not even time to open their mouths. One was caught by the starling, just as he was about to make his bow, and one fell into the ditch with fright, when she looked at him, and was drowned.

"That makes twelve," said the mouse.

"I have not counted them," said the spider. "But now I presume they'll leave me in peace."

"You're a terrible woman," said the mouse. "I prophesy you'll end by going childless to your grave."

For the first time, the spider seemed a little pensive.

"Now her hard heart is melting," said the mouse.

"Oh!" said the wild parsley.

"Ah!" said the goat's-foot.

"Stuff!" said the spider.

But she continued to look pensive and stared at her combs and never noticed that a fly flew into her web. Presently, she said:

"The fact is, one ought at least to see that one brings a pair of strapping wenches into the world. I suppose it's my duty to leave somebody behind me to inherit my contempt for those wretched men."

"She's on the road!" whispered the mouse.

And the goat's-foot and the fool's-parsley nodded and neither of them said a word, so as not to disturb her in her reflections.

But the mouse hurried off to the hedge and called all the surviving gentleman-spiders together:

"The one who proposes to the princess to-morrow gets her," said she. "She's quite altered. She's melted. Her heart is like wax. She won't catch any flies, won't eat, won't drink and just sits and stares wistfully before her. Look sharp!"

Then the mouse ran away.

But the spiders looked at one another doubtfully. Not one of them had the proper courage to risk the attempt, seeing how badly the twelve had fared, and a few even of the wiser ones went up at once and hid under their leaves, so as not to fall into temptation.

A few remained behind, who thought about what the mouse had said, including one little young, thin one, who had always listened while the others were talking about the wonderful princess, but had never said anything himself:

"I think I'll try," he said, suddenly.

"You?" cried all the others, in one breath.

And they began to laugh at the thought that this chap should achieve what so many a bold spider-fellow had lost his life in attempting.

But the little chap let them laugh as much as they pleased:

"I don't suppose I'm poaching on your preserves," he said. "There's none of you that has the pluck. And I just feel like making the experiment. I've been there to look at her and, by Jove, she is a fine woman! If she's rejected the twelve, perhaps she'll accept the thirteenth. Also, I think the suitors went the wrong way to work."

"Oh, you think so, do you?" said the others, still laughing. "And how will you go to work?"

"You can come with me and see for yourselves," he said. "I'll stroll across to-morrow and propose."

5

And he did, the next morning.

He came crawling up on his eight legs, very sedately and circumspectly. A little behind him came all that was left in the way of man-spiders in the hedge. The long twigs on the stubs stretched out their necks to see him. The parsley and the goat's-foot spread out both flowers and leaves, to make his road as easy as possible. The mouse stood on her hind-legs with curiosity and stared and listened.

The princess herself sat in her web and pretended not to see him.

"Noble princess," he said, "I have come to ask you if you will have me for your husband."

"This is the thirteenth," she said.

But within herself she thought that she liked him better than the others. They had all wanted to take her for their wife: this one begged her to take him for her husband. That sounded modest and well-mannered.

"She's giving way," said the mouse and danced with rapture.

"Hush!" said the parsley.

"Hark!" said the goat's-foot.

"She hasn't eaten him yet!" whispered the gentleman-spiders to one another.

"I well know," said the wooer, "how presumptuous it is of me to address such a request to you. What is a wretched man compared with a woman and, in particular, what is a silly fellow like myself to you, who are the largest and cleverest lady in all the hedge? But that is just what attracts me to you."

She turned and looked at him. He nearly fell to the ground with fright and cast his eight eyes down before him. All the other gentleman-spiders rushed away at a furious pace.

"Now she'll eat him," said the goat's-foot and the parsley.

"She is a sweet young thing!" said the twigs on the stubs.

"She's a terrible woman!" said the mouse.

But she did not eat him.

She caught a fly that flew into her web just then and began leisurely to devour it, while attentively contemplating her suitor.

He was an ugly little beggar, especially now, when he was shaking all over his body, because he thought that his last hour had struck. But that was just how she liked to see him. She thought that quite the right attitude for a man. And, when he saw that she gave no sign of making for him, he recovered to such an extent that he was able to finish his speech:

"I quite understand that you can't see anything at all good-looking in me," he said. "I don't want to make myself out better than I am; and I am only a miserable man. But, if I could become the father of a daughter who was like you, I should consider that I had attained the object of my life and give thanks most humbly for my good fortune."

Then a wonderful thing came to pass. She took the leg of a fly and threw it to him, which among spiders means the same as "yes."

Quivering with happiness and apprehension, he crept nearer to her.

"Very well," she said. "I accept you. But mind you don't irritate me. For then I'll eat you."

"She's accepted him!" said the mouse and swooned away with delight.

"She's accepted him!" said the goat's-foot and the parsley.

"She's accepted him!" said the twigs on the stubs and rustled for sheer astonishment.

"She's accepted him!" cried the gentleman-spiders, who had come back, but now ran away again, partly to spread the news in the hedge and partly so as not to be eaten at the wedding.

And it *was* a wedding.

The whole hedge was a scene of jubilation and the mouse was the gladdest of them all, for it was her doing. Or perhaps the fool's-parsley and the goat's-foot were gladder still, for they would now have that family-life in their tops which they had so often longed for and which would raise them to the level of the real bushes. As for the twigs on the old stubs, they were infected with the universal joy and forgot their envy.

The wedding took place forthwith, for there was nothing to wait for. The parsley and the goat's-foot scattered their white flowers on every side to mark the festival. The mouse dragged her little ones up the hedge so that they might see the happy bridal pair; the bluebell rang, the poppy laughed and the bindweed closed her petals half an hour earlier than usual so as not to embarrass the newly-married couple with a misplaced curiosity.

The bride ate all the flies that she had spun up, without offering the bridegroom one. But that did not matter, for he was up to the throat in happiness, so he could not have got a morsel down in any case. He made himself as small as possible. Once, when she stroked him on the back with one of her combs, he shook till they thought that he would die.

6

The mouse was astir early next morning:

"Have you seen nothing of the young couple?" she asked.

"No," said the parsley.

"They're asleep," said the goat's-foot.

"Ah!" said the mouse. "What a good thing that we got her married at last. Now you'll see how sweet and amiable she will become. There is no end to the wonders that love can work. And when the children come!..."

"Do you think she'll sing then?" asked the goat's-foot.

"I shall hope for the best," said the mouse. "She does not look as if she had a voice, but, as I said—love! Now you'll just see, when she comes, what a radiance there will be about her. I half doubt if we shall know her when we see her."

And the mouse laughed and the parsley and the goat's-foot laughed and the sun rose and laughed with the rest.

Then the spider came crawling from under her leafy hiding-place.

"Good luck! Good luck!" squeaked the mouse.

"Good luck! Good luck!" said the parsley and the goat's-foot.

The spider stretched herself and yawned. Then she went off and sat in her web, as though nothing had happened.

"Where's the husband?" asked the mouse. "Won't he get out of bed?"

"I've eaten him this morning," replied the spider.

The mouse gave a scream that was heard all over the hedge. The parsley and the goat's-foot trembled so that all their flowers fell off. The twigs snapped as though a storm were raging.

"He looked so stupid and ugly as he sat there beside me," said the spider; "so I ate him. He could have staid away!"

"Heaven preserve us all!" screamed the mouse. "To eat one's own, lawful husband!"

"Oh dear, oh dear!" said the goat's-foot and the parsley.

"Stuff!" said the spider.

7

That day was very quiet in the hedge and the next was no livelier.

The spider attended to her web and caught and ate more flies than ever. She did not speak a word and looked so fierce that no one dared speak a word to her. The gentleman-spiders took good care not to come near her. They met every evening and talked about it.

"Yes, but he *got* her all the same!" said the most romantic of them.

Then the others fell upon him and asked him if he thought that that was happiness, to be eaten by one's wife on the morning after the wedding. And he didn't know what to answer, for his romance wasn't so very real, after all.

The mouse stole away dejectedly and went to her hole. She took the thing to heart as though it had happened in her own family. The goat's-foot and the parsley hung their screens and felt sheepish and ashamed in the face of the twigs on the stubs. And so great was their overthrow that even the twigs thought it would be a shame to scoff at them.

But, one day, when there was a blazing sun and the spider had crawled as far as she could into the shade of the leaf, the parsley bent down to the mouse's hole and whispered:

"Psst!... Mousie!..."

"What is it?" asked the mouse and came out.

"It's only the goat's-foot and I who have something to ask you," said the parsley. "Tell me—you're so clever—don't you believe that it's possible that the spider may become a different person when she begins to lay her eggs?"

"I believe nothing now," said the mouse. "I shall never believe that that woman will ever lay eggs."

But she did, for all that.

One fine morning, she began and behaved in such a way that no one in the hedge ever forgot the story:

"Ugh!" she said. "That one should be bothered with this nonsense with children now!"

She laid a heap of ten eggs and stood looking at them, angrily.

"Build a nest for your eggs," said the parsley. "All that we have and possess is at your disposal."

"Sit on them and hatch them," said the goat's-foot. "We will weave a roof over you, so the sun won't inconvenience you in the least."

"Lay up some small flies for the children, for when they come out," said the mouse. "You have no idea what those young ones can eat."

"Practise singing to them a bit," said the twigs on the stubs.

"Stuff!" said the spider.

She laid four more heaps. Then she began to spin a fine, close covering of white threads to wrap each heap in separately.

"She's not quite heartless," said the mouse.

The spider took a heap, went down the hedge and buried it in the ground. Then up again for the next heap and so on until all the five heaps were buried.

"There!" she said. "Now that's done with! And they won't catch me at it again. Now at least I am a free and independent woman once more."

"A nice woman!" said the mouse. "A shame and a disgrace to her sex, that's what she is!"

"Such a dear little bird!" said the twigs on the stubs, sarcastically.

But the parsley and the goat's-foot said nothing.

The next morning the spider was gone.

"The starling caught her," said the mouse. "She was gone in a twinkling. I saw it myself."

"If only she doesn't make him ill," said the twigs. "She must have been a bad mouthful."

Then autumn came and winter.

The mouse sat snug in her hole and the spider's eggs lay snug in the ground. The goat's-foot and the parsley withered and died. The twigs on the stubs lost their leaves, but rustled on through storm and frost and snow until next spring.

THE MIST

1

THE sun had just set.

The frog was croaking his even-song, which took so long that there seemed to be no end to it. The bee crept into her hive and the little children cried because it was bed-time. The flowers closed their petals and bent their heads, the bird hid his beak under his wing and the stag lay down to rest in the tall, soft grass of the glade.

The bells of the village-church rang in the night and, when that was done, the old sexton went off home, chatted a little with the villagers who were taking their evening stroll or standing at their doors smoking a pipe, bade them good-night and shut his door.

By and by, it was quite still and darkness fell. There was still a light in the parsonage and at the doctor's. But at the farm-houses it was dark, for the farmers rise early in the summer and therefore have to go early to bed.

Then the stars shone forth in the sky and the moon rose higher and higher. A dog barked down in the village. But he was certainly dreaming, for there was really nothing to bark at.

2

"Is any one here?" asked the mist.

But no one answered, for there was no one there.

So the mist went on in his light, gleaming clothes. He danced over the meadows, up and down, to and fro. Now he would lie quite still for a while and then begin to dance again. He skipped across the pond and into the wood, where he flung his long, wet arms round the trunks of the trees.

"Who are you, friend?" asked the night-scented rocket, who stood and distilled her perfume for her own pleasure.

The mist did not reply, but went on dancing.

"I asked who you were," said the rocket. "And, as you don't answer me, I conclude that you are an ill-mannered churl."

"I'll conclude you!" said the mist.

And he lay down round the night-scented rocket, till her petals were dripping wet.

"Hi! Hi!" screamed the rocket. "Keep your fingers to yourself, my friend! I feel as if I had been dipped in the pond. You needn't be so angry, just because I ask you who you are."

The mist rose up again:

"Who I am?" he repeated. "Why, you wouldn't understand if I told you."

"Try," said the rocket.

"I am the dew-drop on the flowers, the cloud in the sky and the mist on the fields," he answered.

"I beg your pardon?" said the rocket. "Would you mind saying that again? Why, I know the dew-drop. He settles on my petals every morning; and I don't see any resemblance between you."

"Ah, I am the dew-drop, for all that!" said the mist, sadly. "But nobody knows me. I have to spend my life in many shapes. Sometimes I am dew and sometimes I am rain and sometimes I trickle in the form of a clear, cool spring through the wood. But, when I dance over the meadow in the evening, then people say that the mist is rising."

"That's a queer story," said the rocket. "Have you any more to tell me? The night is long and sometimes I feel a little bored."

"It is a sad story," answered the mist. "But you shall hear it if you like."

And he made as though to lie down, but the night-scented rocket shook all her petals in alarm.

"Be so good and keep a little farther off," she said, "at least, until you have introduced yourself properly. I have never cared to be intimate with people whom I don't know."

The mist lay down a few steps away and began his story:

"I was born deep down in the ground," he said, "much deeper than your roots grow. I and my brothers—for you must know that we are a big family—came into the world in the shape of clear crystal spring-water and lay long in our hiding-place. But, one day, we sprang suddenly from under a gentle hill, into the midst of the full, bright sunshine. Believe me, it was delightful to run through the wood. We rippled over the stones and splashed against the banks. Dear little fishes played among us and the trees bent over us and reflected their green splendour. If a leaf fell, we rocked it and caressed it and bore it into the wide world. Oh, how delightful it was! It was really the happiest time in my life."

"Shall I soon hear how you came to be mist?" asked the night-scented rocket, impatiently. "I know the brook. On a very still night, I can hear her babbling from where I stand."

The mist rose and took a little dance across the meadow. Then he came back and continued:

"That is the worst of this world; we are never satisfied with what we have. For instance, we ran on and on until, at last, we came to a big lake, where the water-lilies rocked on the water and the dragon-flies buzzed around on their great stiff wings. On the surface, the water was as clear as a mirror; but, whether we wanted to or not, we had to run along the bottom and there it was dark and dismal. I could not bear it. I longed for the sunbeams. I knew them so well from the time when I ran in the brook. Now they looked down upon us through the leaves and cast a bright light over me. I wanted to see them again and therefore I crept up to the surface and lay down in the sunshine among the white water-lilies and their big green leaves. But oh, how the sun burnt upon the lake! It was almost unendurable and I bitterly regretted that I had not remained at the bottom."

"All this is very dull," said the rocket. "When are we coming to the mist?"

"Here he is!" said the mist and lay down around the flower, who almost lost her breath.

"Hi! Hi!" screamed the rocket. "You're the roughest playfellow I know. Go away and tell your story in your own manner, if you must."

"In the evening, when the sun had gone down, I suddenly became wonderfully light," said the mist. "I don't know how it happened, but I felt that I must rise up and fly away from the lake. And, in fact, before I knew it, I was hovering over the water, away from the dragon-flies and the water-lilies. The evening-wind carried me along; I flew high in the air and there I met many of my brothers, who had been as inquisitive as I and had met with the same fortune. We were wafted up to the sky; we had turned into clouds: do you understand?"

"I am not quite sure," said the rocket. "It does not sound very probable."

"But it's true, for all that," said the mist. "Now listen. The wind carried us for some time through the sky. Then, suddenly, he grew tired of us and let us go. And we fell down upon the earth in pouring rain. The flowers lost no time in closing their petals and the birds took shelter, all except the ducks and geese, who were the better pleased the wetter it was. Oh; and the farmer, too: he stood there rejoicing, because his crops needed rain. He did not care how wet he got. But, otherwise, we really caused a great disturbance."

"Ah, so you're the rain too, are you?" asked the night-scented rocket. "I say, you seem to have plenty to do."

"Yes, I never have any rest," said the mist.

"All the same, I haven't yet heard how you became mist," said the rocket. "Now don't fly into a passion again: you promised to tell me and I would rather hear the whole story over again than once more shiver in your horrid damp arms."

The mist lay and wept for a moment and then continued:

"When I had fallen on the ground as rain, I sank through the black earth and was glad to think I was returning to my native place, the deep subterranean source. There at least I had known peace and been free from cares. But, just as I was sinking, the roots of the trees sucked me up again and, all day long, I had to wander around in the branches and leaves. They used me as a beast of burden, you see. I had to drag up from the roots all the food that the leaves and flowers needed. I was not free until the evening. When the sun had gone down, all the trees and flowers heaved deep sighs and in their sighs my brothers and I were sent forth as a light, gleaming mist. At night, we dance over the fields. But, in the morning, when the sun rises, we turn into beautiful, clear dew-drops and come and hang on your petals. Then you shake us off and we sink deeper and deeper until we come to the source where we were born, unless some root or other snatches us up on the way. And so it goes on: through the brook, into the lake, up in the sky and back again to earth...."

"Stop!" cried the night-scented rocket. "It makes my head swim to listen to you!"

3

Now the frog began to stir. He stretched his legs and went down to the ditch to take his morning bath. The birds began to chirp in the wood and the stag belled among the trees.

Morning began to break and the sun peeped over the hill:

"What's this?" he said. "What does it all mean? One can't see one's hand before one's eyes. Morning-wind! Up with you, you sluggard, and blow that nasty mist away!"

And the morning-wind flew across the fields and blew away the mist. At the same moment, the sun sent his first rays straight down upon the night-scented rocket.

"Hullo!" said the flower. "Here's the sun! Now I must be quick and close my petals. Where in the name of wonder has the mist gone to?"

"Here I am," said the dew-drop hanging from her stalk.

But the night-scented rocket shook her head fretfully:

"Tell that to the children," she said. "I don't believe a word of all you've said. You're just water and nothing more."

"You're right enough there!" said the sun. And he laughed.

THE ANEMONES

1

"PEEWIT! Peewit!" cried the lapwing, as he flew over the moss in the wood. "Dame Spring is coming! I can feel it in my legs and wings."

When the new grass, which lay down below in the earth, heard this, it at once began to sprout and peeped out gaily between the old, yellow straw. For the grass is always in an immense hurry.

Now the anemones in between the trees had also heard the lapwing's cry, but refused on any account to appear above the earth.

"You mustn't believe the lapwing," they whispered to one another. "He is a flighty customer, whom one can't trust. He always comes too early and starts calling at once. No, we will wait quite quietly till the starling and the swallow come. They are sensible, sober people, who are not to be taken in and who know what they are about."

And the starlings came.

They sat down on a twig outside their summer villa and looked about them.

"Too early, as usual," said Mr. Starling. "Not a green leaf and not a fly, except an old tough one of last year, not worth opening one's beak for."

Mrs. Starling said nothing, but looked none too cheerful either.

"If we had only remained in our snug winter-quarters beyond the mountains!" said Mr. Starling. He was angry because his wife did not answer, for he was so cold that he thought a little discussion might do him good. "But it's *your* fault, just as last year. You're always in such a terrible hurry to go to the country."

"If I'm in a hurry, I know the reason *why*," said Mrs. Starling. "And it would be a shame for you if you didn't know too, for they are your eggs as well as mine."

"Heaven forbid!" replied Mr. Starling, indignantly. "When have I denied my family? Perhaps you expect me, over and above, to sing to you in the cold?"

"Yes, *that* I do!" said Mrs. Starling, in the tone which he could not resist.

He at once began to whistle as best he could. But, when Mrs. Starling had heard the first notes, she flapped her wings and pecked at him with her beak:

"Will you be quiet at once!" she screamed, angrily. "That sounds so dismal that it makes one quite melancholy. You'd better see to it that the anemones come out. I think it's high time. And, besides, one always feels warmer when there are others shivering too."

Now, as soon as the anemones had heard the starling's first whistle, they carefully stuck their heads out of the ground. But they were still so tightly tucked up in their green wraps that one could hardly see them. They looked like green buds which might turn into anything.

"It's too early," they whispered. "It's a shame for the starling to call us. There's no one in the world left that one can trust."

Then the swallow came:

"Tsee! Tsee!" he whistled and darted through the air on his long, pointed wings. "Out with you, you silly flowers! Can't you see that Dame Spring has come?"

But the anemones had become careful. They just pushed their green wraps a little to one side and peeped out:

"One swallow does not make a summer," they said. "Where is your wife? You have only come to see if it's possible to live here and now you're trying to take us in. But we are not so stupid as all that. We know that, if once we catch cold, we're done for."

"You're a pack of poltroons," said the swallow and sat down on the weathercock on the ranger's roof and looked out over the landscape.

But the anemones stood and waited and were very cold. One or two of them, who could not control their impatience, cast off their wraps in the sun. The cold killed them at night and the story of their pitiful death went from flower to flower and aroused great consternation.

2

Then Dame Spring came, one delightfully mild and still night.

No one knows what she looks like, for no one has ever seen her. But all long for her and thank her and bless her. She goes through the wood and touches the flowers and the trees and they bud at once. She goes through the stables and unfastens the animals and lets them out into the field. She goes straight into men's hearts and makes them glad. She makes it difficult for the best-behaved boy to sit still on his bench at school and occasions a terrible lot of mistakes in the exercise-books.

But she does not do this all at once. She attends to her business night after night and comes first to those who long for her most.

So it happened that, on the very night when she arrived, she went straight off to the anemones, who stood in their green wraps and could no longer curb their impatience.

And one, two, three! There they stood in newly-ironed white frocks and looked so fresh and pretty that the starlings sang their finest songs for sheer joy at the sight of them.

"Oh, how lovely it is here!" said the anemones. "How warm the sun is! And how the birds sing! It is a thousand times better than last year."

But they say this every year, so it doesn't count.

Now there were many others who went quite off their heads when they saw that the anemones were out. There was a schoolboy who wanted to have his summer holidays then and there and then there was the beech, who was most offended.

"Aren't you coming to me soon, Dame Spring?" he said. "I am a much more important person than those silly anemones and really I can no longer control my buds."

"I'm coming, I'm coming!" replied Dame Spring. "But you must give me a little time."

She went on through the wood. And, at every step, more anemones appeared. They stood in thick bevies round the roots of the beech and bashfully bowed their round heads to the ground.

"Look up freely," said Dame Spring, "and rejoice in heaven's bright sun. Your lives are but short, so you must enjoy them while they last."

The anemones did as she told them. They stretched themselves and spread their white petals to every side and drank as much sunshine as they could. They knocked their heads against one another and wound their stalks together and laughed and were constantly happy.

"Now I can wait no longer," said the beech and came into leaf.

Leaf after leaf crept out of its green covering and spread out and fluttered in the wind. The whole green crown arched itself like a mighty roof above the ground.

"Good heavens, is it evening so soon?" asked the anemones, who thought that it had turned quite dark.

"No, it is *death*," said Dame Spring. "Now *you're* finished. It's the same with you as with the best in this world. All must bud, blossom and die."

"Die?" cried some of the small anemones. "Must we die yet?"

And some of the large anemones turned quite red in the face with anger and pride:

"We know all about it!" they said. "It's the beech that's killing us. He steals the sunshine for his own leaves and grudges us a single ray. He is a nasty, wicked thing."

They stood and scolded and wept for some days. Then Dame Spring came for the last time through the wood. She had still the oaks and some other querulous old fellows to visit:

"Lie down nicely to sleep now in the ground," she said to the anemones. "It is no use kicking against the pricks. Next year, I will come again and wake you to new life."

And some of the anemones did as she told them. But others continued to stick their heads in the air and grew up so ugly and lanky that they were horrid to look at.

"Fie, for shame!" they cried to the beech-leaves. "It's you that are killing us."

But the beech shook his long boughs, so that the brown husks fell to the ground.

"Wait till the autumn, you little blockheads," he said and laughed. "Then you'll just see."

The anemones could not understand what he meant. But, when they had stretched themselves as far as they could, they cracked in two and withered.

3

The summer was past and the farmer had carted his corn home from the field.

The wood was still green, but darker; and, in many places, yellow and red leaves appeared among the green ones. The sun was tired of his warm work during the summer and went early to bed.

At night, the winter stole through the trees to see if his time would soon come. When he found a flower, he kissed her politely and said:

"Well, well, are you there still? I am glad to see you. Stay where you are. I am a harmless old man and wouldn't hurt a fly."

But the flower shuddered with his kiss and the bright dew-drops that hung from her petals froze to ice at the same moment.

The winter went oftener and oftener through the wood. He breathed upon the leaves, so that they turned yellow, or upon the ground, so that it grew hard.

Even the anemones, who lay down below in the earth and waited for Dame Spring to come again as she had promised, could feel his breath and shuddered right down to their roots.

"Oh dear, how cold it is!" they said to one another. "How ever shall we last through the winter? We are sure to die before it is over."

"Now *my* time has come," said the winter. "Now I need no longer steal round like a thief in the night. From to-morrow I shall look everybody straight in the face and bite his nose and make his eyes run with tears."

At night the storm broke loose.

"Let me see you make a clean sweep of things," said the winter.

And the storm obeyed his orders. He tore howling through the wood and shook the branches so that they creaked and broke. Any that were at all decayed fell down and those that held on had to twist and turn to every side.

"Away with all that finery!" howled the storm and tore off the leaves. "This is no time to deck one's self out. Soon there will be snow on the branches: that's another story."

All the leaves fell terrified to the ground, but the storm did not let them be in peace. He took them by the waist and waltzed with them over the field, high up in the air and into the wood again, swept them together into great heaps and scattered them once more to every side, just as the fit seized him.

Not until the morning did the storm grow weary and go down.

"Now you can have peace for *this* time," he said. "I am going down till we have our spring-cleaning. Then we can have another dance, if there are any of you left by that time."

And then the leaves went to rest and lay like a thick carpet over the whole earth.

The anemones felt that it had grown delightfully warm.

"I wonder if Dame Spring can have come yet?" they asked one another.

"I haven't got my buds ready!" cried one of them.

"No more have I! No more have I!" exclaimed the others in chorus.

But one of them took courage and just peeped out above the ground.

"Good-morning!" cried the withered beech-leaves. "It's rather too early, little missie: if only you don't come to any harm!"

"Isn't that Dame Spring?" asked the anemone.

"Not just yet," replied the beech-leaves. "It's we, the green leaves you were so angry with in the summer. Now we have lost our green color and have not much left to make a show of. We have enjoyed our youth and danced, I may tell you. And now we are lying here and protecting all the little flowers in the ground against the winter."

"And meanwhile I am standing and freezing with my bare branches," said the beech, crossly.

The anemones talked about it down in the earth and thought it very nice.

"Those dear beech-leaves!" they said.

"Mind you remember it next summer, when I come into leaf," said the beech.

"We will, we will!" whispered the anemones.

For that sort of thing is promised; but the promise is never kept.

THE QUEEN BEE

1

THE farmer opened his bee-hive.

"Out with you!" he said. "The sun is shining; the flowers are blossoming everywhere and are a sheer joy to behold. Let me see you industrious now and gather me a good lot of honey which I can sell to the shopkeeper in the autumn. Many mickles make a muckle; and you know that things are looking bad with agriculture."

"What is agriculture to us?" said the bees.

But they flew out nevertheless, for they had been in the hive all winter and were longing for a breath of fresh air. Buzzing and humming, they stretched their legs and tried their wings. They swarmed forth everywhere, crawled up and down the hive, flew off to the flowers and shrubs and walked about on the ground.

There were many hundred bees.

The queen came last. She was bigger than the others and it was she that reigned in the hive.

"Stop that nonsense now, children," she said, "and begin to do something. A decent bee does not idle, but turns to, in a capable way, and makes good use of her time."

Then she divided them into companies and set them to work.

"You, there, fly out and see if there is any honey in the flowers. The second company can gather pollen; and, when you come home, deliver it all nicely to the old bees indoors."

They flew away. But all the young ones were still left. They formed the last company, for they had never been out before.

"What are *we* to do?" they asked.

"You? You've got to *sweat!*" said the queen. "One, two, three and to work!"

And they sweated as best they knew how and the loveliest yellow wax burst out of their bodies.

"That's right," said the queen. "Now we will begin to build."

The old bees took the wax and started building a number of small hexagonal cells, all alike and close together. All the time that they were building, the others came flying up with pollen and honey, which they laid at the queen's feet.

"Now we'll knead the dough!" said she. "But first pour a little honey in; then it will taste better."

They kneaded and kneaded and made nice little loaves of bee-bread, which they carried to the cells.

"Now we'll go on building!" commanded the queen-bee. And they sweated wax and built away with a vengeance.

"I may as well begin my own work," said the queen and heaved a deep sigh, for this was the hardest of all.

She sat down in the middle of the hive and began to lay eggs. She laid great heaps and the bees ran up, took the little eggs in their mouths and carried them into the new cells. Every egg got its own little room; and, when they were all disposed of, the queen ordered the bees to put doors to the cells and to shut them tight.

"Good!" she said, when they had finished. "Now you can build me ten big, handsome rooms at the outer edge of the hive."

The bees did so in a trice and then the queen laid ten beautiful eggs, one in each of the big rooms, and put a door before them.

Every day, the bees flew out and in and gathered great heaps of honey and pollen; but, in the evening, when their work was done, they set the doors a little ajar and peeped in at the eggs.

"Take care!" said the queen, one day. "Now they're coming!"

And suddenly all the eggs burst and in each cell lay a nice little baby.

"What queer creatures!" said the young bees. "Why, they have no eyes; and where are their legs and wings?"

"Those are grubs," said the queen, "and that's what you young green-horns yourselves once looked like. You have to be a grub before you can become a proper bee. Hurry now and give them something to eat."

The bees hastened to feed the little young ones; but they did not all fare equally well. The ten that lay in the large rooms got as much to eat as ever they wanted and a big helping of honey was carried in to them every day.

"Those are princesses," said the queen. "Therefore, you must treat them well. The others you can stint in their food; they are only work-people and must accustom themselves to take things as they come."

And the poor little creatures got a small piece of bee-bread every morning and nothing more; they had to be content with that, even though they were ever so hungry.

2

In one of the small hexagonal cells close to the princesses' rooms lay a tiny little grub. She was the youngest of them all and had but quite lately come out of the egg. She could not see, but she could distinctly hear the grown-up bees talking outside; and meanwhile she lay quite still and just thought her own thoughts.

"I could do with a little more to eat," she said and tapped at her door.

"You've got enough for today," replied the old bee who crawled up and down outside in the passage and had been appointed head-nurse to the baby bees.

"Ah, but I'm hungry!" cried the little grub. "And then I want to have a princess's room; I feel so cramped in here."

"Oh, just listen to her!" said the old bee, sarcastically. "One would think she was a dainty little princess by the pretensions she puts forward! You were born to toil and drudge, my little friend. A common working-bee, that's what you are; and you'll never be anything else in all your days."

"Ah, but I want to be a queen!" said the grub and thumped on the door.

The old bee, of course, made no reply to such silly trash, but went on to the others. Everywhere they were crying for more food; and the little grub could hear it all.

"It's really hard," she thought, "that we should be so hungry."

And then she tapped on the wall and called to the princess on the other side:

"Give me a little of your honey! Let me come in to you in your room. I am lying here and starving and I am quite as good as you."

"Ah, you just wait till I'm queen-regnant!" said the princess. "Be sure I shan't forget your impudence."

But she had hardly said this before the other princesses began to bawl most terribly:

"You shan't be queen! *I* will! *I* will!" they all yelled together and began to thump on the walls and make a frightful din.

The head-nurse came running up at once and opened the doors:

"What are your Royal Highnesses' commands?" she asked and curtseyed and scraped with her legs.

"More honey!" they all cried together. "But me first, me first! I'm going to be queen!"

"This minute, this minute, your Royal Highnesses!" she replied and ran off as fast as her six old legs could carry her.

Soon after, she came back with several other bees. They dragged a quantity of honey with them, which they put down the throats of the angry little princesses, till gradually they grew quiet and all ten of them went to sleep.

But the little grub lay awake and thought over what had happened. She was yearning for honey and shook the door:

"Give me some honey! I can stand this no longer; I'm quite as good as the others."

The old bee told her to be silent:

"Keep still, you little squaller! Here comes the queen."

And the queen-bee came as she spoke:

"Go away," she said to the bees. "I wish to be alone."

She stood long, silently, outside the princesses' rooms.

"You're lying in there now and sleeping," she said at last. "Eat and sleep, that's what you do, from morn till night, and, every day that passes, you grow stronger and fatter. In a few days, you will be full-grown and you will creep out of the cells. Then my time is over. I know it well! I have heard the bees saying among themselves that they want a younger and prettier queen; and then they will drive me away in disgrace. But that I will not submit to. To-morrow, I shall kill them all, so that I can go on reigning till I die."

Then she went away, but the little grub had heard all that she said.

"Goodness gracious!" she thought. "After all, it's really a pity for the little princesses. They certainly give themselves airs and they have been nasty to me; but it would be sad, for all that, if the wicked queen killed them. I think I shall tell the old grumbler in the passage."

Then she began to tap at the door again; and the old head-nurse came running up; but this time she was really angry:

"Now, you had better mind yourself, my good grub!" she said. "You're the youngest of them all and the noisiest. Next time, I'll report you to the queen."

"Ah, but first listen to me," said the grub; and then she betrayed the queen's wicked plan.

"Heavens above! Is that true?" cried the old bee and struck her wings together with horror.

And, without listening to any more, she hurried away to tell the other bees.

"I do think I deserve a little honey for my goodwill," said the little grub. "But now I can go to sleep with an easy conscience."

The next morning, the queen, when she thought that all the bees were in bed, came to put the princesses to death. The grub could hear her talking aloud to herself; but was very frightened of the wicked queen and hardly dared move.

"If only she doesn't kill the princesses," she thought and crept closer to the door to hear what was happening.

The queen-bee looked carefully round in every direction and opened the first of the doors. But, as she did so, the bees swarmed up from every side, seized her by the legs and wings and dragged her away.

"What does this mean?" she screamed. "Are you rising in rebellion?"

"No, your Majesty," replied the bees, respectfully, "but we know that you are thinking of killing the princesses; and that you cannot possibly be permitted to do. How should we manage in that case in the autumn, when your Majesty dies?"

"Unhand me!" screamed the queen and tried to tear herself free. "I am still queen and have the right to do what I please. How do you know that I shall die in the autumn?"

But the bees held fast and dragged her out of the hive. There they let her go; but she shook her wings with rage and said:

"You are disloyal subjects, who are not worth reigning over. I will not stay here another hour, but will go away and build a new hive. Are there any of you that will follow me?"

Some of the old bees who had been grubs with the queen declared that they would go with her, and soon after they flew away.

"Now we have no queen," said the others. "We shall have to take good care of the princesses."

And so they stuffed them with honey from morning till night and the princesses grew and thrived and squabbled and made more and more noise day after day.

And no one gave a thought to the little grub.

3

One morning, the doors of the princesses' rooms flew open and they all ten came out as beautiful full-grown queen-bees; the other bees came running up and looked at them with admiration.

"Oh, how lovely they are!" they said. "It is not easy to say which of them is the prettiest."

"I am!" cried one.

"You make a great mistake!" said the second and thrust at her with her sting.

"You flatter yourselves!" cried the third. "I should think I am no less beautiful than you."

Soon they were all screaming together; and, a little later, they all began to fight. The bees wanted to part them, but the old head-nurse said:

"Just let them fight, then we shall see which is the strongest and we will elect her to be our queen. After all, we can't have more than one."

The bees then formed a ring and watched the combat. It was long and hard-fought. Wings and legs were bitten off and flew around in the air; and, after some time, eight of the princesses lay dead on the ground. The last two went on fighting for a long while. One had lost all her wings and the other had only four legs left.

"It will be a pitiful queen, whichever of them we get," said one of the bees. "We had better have kept the old one."

But she might as well have saved herself the observation, for at that very moment the princesses suddenly gave each other so violent a thrust with their stings that both of them fell stone-dead.

"Here's a nice thing!" cried the bees and they all ran about in consternation. "Now we have no queen! What shall we do? What shall we do?"

They crept round the hive in utter bewilderment and despair. But the oldest and wisest of them sat in a corner and held counsel. They discussed at length what expedient they should resort to in this unfortunate case; but at last the head-nurse spoke and said:

"Now I will tell you how you can get out of the dilemma, if you will follow my advice. I remember that the same misfortune once happened long ago in this hive. I was a grub at the time and I lay in my cell and distinctly heard what was going on. All the princesses had killed one another and the old queen had gone away, just as now. But then the bees took one of us grubs and put her in one of the princesses' cells. They fed her every day on the best and finest honey that the hive contained; and, when she was full-grown, she was a really good and beautiful queen. I remember the whole story clearly, for I thought at the time that they might just as well have taken me. But never mind that at present. I propose that we should behave in just the same way."

The bees gladly cried that they agreed, and they ran straight off to fetch a grub.

"Stop a bit," cried the head-nurse, "and take me with you. After all, I have managed to help you. Now, look here: it must be one of the youngest grubs, for she must have time to think of her new position. When you've been brought up to be a common worker, it's not so easy to accustom yourself to wear a crown."

The bees thought this sensible too, and the old bee continued:

"Just beside the princesses' rooms lies a little grub. She is the youngest of them all. She must have learned a deal from hearing the princesses' cultured conversation; and I have noticed that she is not without character. Moreover, it was she who had the honesty to tell me of the old queen's wicked thoughts. Let us take her."

They all went forthwith, in a solemn procession, to the narrow, hexagonal cell in which the little grub lay. The head-nurse knocked politely at the door, opened it carefully and told the grub what the bees had decided upon. At first she almost refused to believe her own ears; but, when they carried her carefully into one of the beautiful large rooms and brought her as much honey as she could eat, she saw that it was serious.

"So I am to be queen after all!" she said to the head-nurse. "You never thought that, you old grumbler!"

"I hope your Majesty will forget my rude remarks at the time when you lay in the hexagonal cell," said the old bee and dropped a respectful curtsey.

"I forgive you!" replied the new-fledged princess. "Get me some more honey!"

Soon after, the grub was full-grown and stepped out of her room, looking as large and beautiful as the bees could possibly wish. And she did know how to command and no mistake!

"Away with you!" she said. "We want more honey for winter use and you others must sweat more wax. I mean to build a wing to the hive. The new princesses will live in it next year; it is much too unpleasant for them to be so near the common grubs."

"What next!" cried the bees to one another. "One would really think that she had been queen from the time when she lay in the egg!"

"No," said the head-nurse, "that she was not. But she has had *queenly thoughts*; and that is the great thing."

THE CATERPILLAR

1

THE whole kitchen-garden was full of caterpillars and one of them was bigger than the others. Day after day, he crawled about on a head of cabbage just at the edge of the walk. He was stout and fat and so green that it hurt one's eyes to look at him. He ate and ate, positively did nothing else but eat.

"You stupid beast!" said the gardener. "You and your brothers and sisters eat up half my cabbage. If there were not so many of you, I would kill you."

"The stupid beast!" sang the nightingale who sat in the syringa-bush. "He does not care about flowers or music and singing. Nothing but eat, eat, eat!"

"The stupid beast!" piped the swallow who swept over the kitchen-garden on his long, pointed wings. "He has not the smallest taste for poetry: never thinks of sunshine and summer air. There is not the least go in him. Nothing but eat, eat, eat! And then, into the bargain, he is so full of loathsome poisonous hairs that one can't eat him one's self."

"The stupid beast!" snapped the ant, who ran past with a grain of corn in her mouth. "Does he ever think of house and home? Of his children? Of food for the winter? Nothing but eat, eat, eat!"

"Goodness me!" said the caterpillar.

And he said no more for the time being, so overpowered was he with all this scolding. But, all the while that he was eating the green, juicy cabbage, he pondered on what he had heard and most on what the ant had said. And, when the ant next came by, the caterpillar had made it out:

"Hi, you ant!" he cried. "Stop a bit and explain to me what you said about the children. Don't you know that I am a child myself? I only want time in order to grow big and pretty."

The ant stood still and dropped the grain of corn she had in her mouth, so great was her amazement:

"Are *you* a child?" she asked. "A nice child you are! Why, you're a perfect elephant, fifty times as big as myself. And so you're a child, are you? Lord knows what you'll look like when you're grown up!"

"I don't know for certain," said the caterpillar, with an air of mystery. "But I have a suspicion. If I could only tell you what I sometimes notice inside myself! I am quite certain that I shall be something great one day—if only you give me time to grow. I shall fly away over the garden on beautiful wings; I shall be a butterfly: just you wait and see! I know by my dreams that I am related to you others and that I am quite as good as you."

"Bah!" said the ant and spat on the ground. "It is simply disgusting to listen to such balderdash. Dreams? Suspicions? No, there's a thing that's called the family and the ant-hill: that's what *I* stick to. Good-bye, you stupid caterpillar."

Then she ran off, but stopped a little farther away and once more said:

"Bah!"

And the sun blazed and the caterpillar basked in its rays while he ate the green cabbage.

2

It was now past mid-day and the nightingale in the syringa-bush could not bear to sing in so great a heat. So he stopped and took an afternoon nap. The swallow flew up aloft to get a breath of fresh air, the ant carried her little white eggs up into the sun and the gardener sat under the big walnut-tree and had his dinner with his wife and children.

But the caterpillar went on eating indefatigably.

Suddenly a multitude of small black dots appeared in the air over the kitchen-garden. They danced up and down and up and down. At last, they hung low down, just above the caterpillar, and he could see that they were nice little animals, with fine, bright wings.

"Who are you? What do you want?" asked the caterpillar.

"We are mothers," replied the little animals, "and we have come out to look for a place for our children."

"Well, that's right and proper enough," said the caterpillar, who was thinking of what the ant had said. "But I don't like you, for all that."

"That's very sad," said the animalcules, "for we just happen to be so awfully fond of you."

And, at that moment, a number of them settled on the caterpillar's back.

"Oh! Oh!" he screamed. "Murder! Help! Police!"

The little animals flew up again, but remained hovering in the air above the caterpillar.

"But who are you?" he asked and writhed with pain. "What have I done to you that you should ill-treat me so?"

"Every one provides for himself and his," replied the animalcules, "and we have now provided for our children. We are parasitic flies and our name is Ichneumon: it is not a pretty one, but it happens to be the best we have. For the rest, we are relations of the ants, if you happen to know them."

"It's a good enough family," said the caterpillar and sighed. "But I don't know why everybody should scold at me and sting me and scoff at me. What is this that you have done to me now?"

"You'll know soon enough," said the ichneumons. "Good-bye for the present and thank you."

Then they soared up aloft and became little black dots again and, at last, disappeared altogether.

But the caterpillar heaved long and deep sighs and ate twice as much cabbage to console himself. Nevertheless, he could not keep from thinking of the uncomfortable visit he had had:

"I have a suspicion," he said to himself. "An awkward suspicion. If only I could make something of it!"

3

But, when some time had passed, he began to make something of it.

He simply could not satisfy his appetite any longer. The more he ate, the hungrier he became. He munched one piece of cabbage-leaf after another and, nevertheless, he felt quite faint with hunger.

"What is the meaning of *this* now?" he said, despondently.

"It's we!" answered something inside him.

"Eh? What?" said the caterpillar and rolled round with terror. "Am I haunted inside, or have I gone mad?"

"It's we, it's the ichneumon-flies' young," came the sound again from deep down in his stomach.

The caterpillar's head was in a whirl. But, when he had collected himself a little, he began to understand:

"So the ichneumons laid their eggs in my body!" he cried, in despair. "And have I now to feed all their voracious young?"

"That's it!" said the young ones. "You've hit it to a T. Bestir yourself now, you stupid, lazy caterpillar, and eat till you burst, or we'll eat you!"

So saying, they took a good nip at his flesh.

"Oh, oh!" yelled the caterpillar. "I will, I will, indeed I will."

"Yes, but hurry up!" said the young ones. "We are so hungry, so hungry!"

And the caterpillar ate ever so much more than before, but it was not the slightest use. He could never eat enough and the ichneumon-flies' young kept on crying for more. The ant and the swallow and the nightingale mocked at him every day and the gardener beat the cabbage with his rake, so angry was he at all this consumption.

But the caterpillar swallowed it all and reflected that there was not on earth a lot so distressing as his.

"Jeer away!" he thought. "You're quick at that. If only you knew that I don't get the food myself which I procure: the benefit of it all goes to the ichneumon-flies' young."

He ate and ate desperately. At last, he could bear it no longer. All day long, he noticed how the ichneumons were rummaging about inside him. He rolled round on the cabbage-leaf in despair and turned and twisted and screamed for help.

"Rather eat me up altogether while you're about it!" he cried. "Rather let me die at once: I can't endure this life!"

"Tut, tut!" said the young ones inside him and cackled with laughter. "It's not so easy as that. You'll be eaten right enough, when the time comes, never fear! But, for the present, all you have to do is to hold your tongue and eat."

4

Every day, the young ones grew bigger and wanted more food. When they could no longer satisfy themselves with what the caterpillar ate, they began to devour two large lumps of fat which he had saved up in the happy days before the ichneumons came. They were meant to be used for wings and legs, once he had become a butterfly. And, when he noticed that they were gone, he shed bitter tears:

"Alas for my beautiful dreams!" he said. "Now I shall never be a butterfly, never flit in the sun all over the garden."

"I told you all the time that that was nonsense about the butterfly," said the ant, who passed at that moment.

"Listen," said the caterpillar. "If you have a heart beating in your body, then help me, Ant."

Then he told her of his misfortune. The swallow and the nightingale came and listened and the caterpillar implored them for advice and assistance.

"After all, I'm of your race," he ended by saying. "Believe me, I feel it. If I get time and leisure, I shall turn into something pretty, a butterfly. I have felt that inside myself since the time when I was quite little."

The swallow and the nightingale looked at each other and shook their heads. But the ant, who was the cleverest of the three, nodded thoughtfully and then said:

"What you say about the relationship may have something in it. To a certain extent. For we are all poor mortals, as the gardener says. But that bit about the butterfly is positively nothing but imagination. I am sorry for you, goodness knows I am, but I can't help you. You must bear your lot with patience."

"I *can't* bear it!" cried the caterpillar. "It is killing me. Think of the butterflies: are they not beautiful? Don't you like looking at them? Help me, do you hear! If I die, a butterfly dies. Only think, if one day there were no butterflies!"

"Well," said the ant, "as for that, the world would go on, even if you are right. There are caterpillars enough in the garden and, if you really *are* butterflies' children, there would be plenty left, even though a few did get lost. However, I have no time to speculate on this folly. If you wish to have my opinion in a nutshell, here it is, that your mother must have looked after you foolishly, for you to fall into the ichneumons' power like this. And now I must go home and look after *my* children. Good-bye and bless you!"

Then the ant went away. The nightingale flew up into the bush and sang in the warm evening so that all had to listen and admire him and the swallow soared high into the air and prophesied fine weather for the morrow.

But the caterpillar crouched humbly over his cabbage-leaf and ate.

5

"I think there are too many of us in here," said one of the ichneumon-grubs the next morning. "I can't breathe."

"There's a way out of that," said one of the others. "Let's bite a hole in the creature's air-ducts; then we'll get air enough. But see that he has one or two left, or we shall risk his going and suffocating before his time."

It was no sooner said than done. But the caterpillar screamed louder than ever.

"Air! Air! I shall die of suffocation!"

"No, you won't," replied the young ones. "But you had better accustom yourself to be content with little. Hurry back to the cabbage."

"Now it's all up with me," said the caterpillar, one morning.

"You may be right, this time," replied the ichneumon-grubs.

That evening, they ate the last remnant of their host. Only the skin was left of the dead caterpillar. It lay dry and shrivelled up outside the grubs, who nestled in it as in a warm fur.

One fine day, they flew out. Pretty little animals they were, with light, bright wings, like their parents.

"Hurrah!" they cried. "Now it's only a question of finding a caterpillar for our young. Each for himself and the devil take the hindmost: such is nature's law. We are nature's police: we see to it that things keep their balance. It would be a hideous world indeed, if it were full of caterpillars!"

"Or of ichneumon-flies!" piped the swallow and gulped down a mouthful of them as he spoke.

THE BEECH AND THE OAK

1

IT was in the old days.

There were no towns with houses and streets and towering church-steeples. There were no schools. For there were not many boys and those there were learnt from their fathers to shoot with a bow and arrow, to hunt the deer in his hiding-place, to kill bears in order to make clothes of their hides and to get fire by rubbing two pieces of wood together. When they knew all this thoroughly, their education was completed.

Nor were there any railways, or tilled fields, or ships on the sea, or books, for there was nobody who would read them.

There was hardly anything but trees.

But then of trees there were plenty. They stood everywhere, from coast to coast, mirrored themselves in every river and sea and stretched their mighty branches up into the sky. They stooped out over the sea-shore, dipped their branches in the black water of the marshes and looked out haughtily over the land from the tall hills.

They all knew one another, for they belonged to one big family and they were proud of it.

"We are all oak-trees," they said and drew themselves up. "We own the land and we govern it."

And they were quite right, for there were only very few people at that time. Otherwise there was nothing but wild animals. Bears, wolves and foxes went hunting, while the deer grazed by the edge of the marsh. The wood-mouse sat outside her hole eating acorns and the beaver built his ingenious house on the river-bank.

2

Then, one day, the bear came trudging along and lay down at full length under a great oak-tree.

"Are you there again, you robber?" said the oak and shook a heap of withered leaves over him.

"You really ought not to be so wasteful with your leaves, old friend," said the bear, licking his paws. "They are the only thing you have to keep off the sun with."

"If you don't like me, you can go away," replied the oak, proudly. "I am lord of the land and, look where you may, you will find none but my brothers."

"True enough," growled the bear. "That's just the tiresome part of it. I've been for a little trip abroad, you see, and have been a bit spoilt. That was in a country down south. I there took a nap under the beech-trees. Those are tall, slender trees, not crooked old fellows like you. And their tops are so close that the sunbeams can't pierce through them at all. It was a real delight to sleep there of an afternoon, believe me."

"Beech-trees?" asked the oak, curiously. "What are they?"

"You might wish that you were half as handsome as a beech-tree," said the bear. "But now I'm not going to gossip with you any more. I've had to trot over a mile in front of a confounded hunter, who caught me on one of my hind-legs with an arrow. Now I want to sleep; and perhaps you will be so kind as to provide me with rest, since you can't provide me with shade."

The bear lay down and closed his eyes, but there was no sleep for him this time. For the other trees had heard what he had said and there came such a chattering and a jabbering and a rustling of leaves as had never been known in the forest.

"Heaven knows what sort of trees those are!" said the one. "Of course, it's a story which the bear wants us to swallow," said another.

"What can trees be like whose leaves are so close together that the sunbeams can't pierce through them?" asked a little oak who had been listening to what the big ones were saying.

But next to him stood an old, gnarled tree, who slapped the little oak on the head with one of his lower branches.

"Hold your tongue," he said, "and don't talk till you've got something to say. And you others need not believe a word of the bear's nonsense. I am much taller than you and I can see a long way over the forest. But as far away as I can see there is nothing but oak-trees."

The little oak remained sheepish and silent and the other big trees whispered softly to one another, for they had a great respect for the old one.

But the bear got up and rubbed his eyes.

"Now you have disturbed my afternoon nap," he growled, angrily, "and I shall have my revenge on you, never fear. When I come back, I shall bring some beech-seed with me and I'll answer for it that you will all turn yellow with envy when you see how handsome the new trees are."

Then he trotted away. But the oaks talked to one another for days at a time of the queer trees which he had told them of.

"If they come, we'll do for them!" said the little oak-tree.

But the old oak gave him one on the head:

"If they come, you shall be civil to them, you puppy," he said. "But they won't come."

3

Now this was where the old oak was wrong, for they did come.

In the autumn, the bear returned and lay down under the old oak.

"I am to give you the kind regards of the people down below there," he said and picked some funny little things off his shaggy hide. "Just look what I've got for you."

"What's that?" asked the oak.

"That's beech," replied the bear. "Beech-seed, as I promised you."

Then he trampled them into the earth and prepared to leave again:

"It's a pity that I can't stay to see how annoyed you will be," he said, "but those confounded human beings have become so offensive. They killed my wife and one of my brothers the other day and I must look out for a place where I can dwell in peace. There is hardly a spot left for an honest bear to live in. Good-bye, you gnarled old oak-trees."

When the bear had jogged off, the trees looked at one another seriously.

"Let us now see what happens," said the old oak.

And thereupon they betook themselves to rest. The winter came and tore all their leaves from them. The snow lay high over all the land and every tree stood plunged in his own thoughts and dreamt of spring.

And, when the spring came, the grass was green and the birds began to sing where they last left off. The flowers swarmed up out of the ground and everything looked fresh and vigorous.

The oaks alone still stood with leafless branches:

"It is very distinguished to come last," they said to one another. "The king of the forest does not arrive before the whole company is assembled."

But at last they did arrive. All the leaves burst forth from the fat buds and the trees looked at one another and complimented one another on their good appearance. The little oak had grown a decent bit. This made him feel important and think that he now had the right to join in the conversation:

"There's not much coming of the bear's beech-trees," he said, mockingly, but at the same time glanced up anxiously at the old oak who used to slap his head.

The old oak heard what he said and so did the others. But they said nothing. None of them had forgotten what the bear had said and every morning, when the sun shone, they peeped down secretly to see if the beeches had come. At bottom they were a little anxious, but they were too proud to talk about it.

And, one day, at last, the little sprouts shot up from the ground. The sun shone upon them and the rain fell over them, so that it was not long before they grew to a good height.

"I say, how pretty they are!" said the great oaks and twisted their crooked branches still more, so as to see them better.

"You are welcome among us," said the old oak and gave them a gracious nod. "You shall be my foster-children and have just as good a time as my own."

"Thank you," said the little beeches and not a word more.

But the little oak did not like the strange trees:

"It's awful, the way you're shooting up," he said, in a vexed tone. "You're already half as tall as I am. May I beg you to remember that I am much older than you and of a good family besides?"

The beeches laughed with their tiny little green leaves, but said nothing.

"Shall I bend my branches a little to one side, so that the sun can shine on you better?" asked the old tree, politely.

"Much obliged," replied the beeches. "We can grow quite nicely in the shade."

4

And all that summer passed and another summer and still more. The beeches went on growing steadily and at last grew right over the little oak's head.

"Keep your leaves to yourselves!" cried the oak. "You're standing in my light; and that I can't endure. I must have proper sunshine. Take your leaves away, else I shall die."

The beeches only laughed and went on growing. At last, they met right above the little oak's head and then he died.

"That was ill done!" roared the big oaks and shook their branches in anger.

But the old oak stood up for his foster-children.

"Serve him right!" he said. "That's the reward of his bragging. I say it, although he is my own flesh and blood. But you must be careful now, you little beeches, for else I shall slap you on the head too."

5

The years passed and the beeches kept on growing and gradually became slim young trees that reached right up among the old oak's branches.

"You're beginning to be rather intrusive for my taste," said the old oak. "You had better try to grow a bit thicker and give up shooting into the air like that. Just look how your branches stick out. Bend them decently, as you see us do. How will you manage when a regular storm comes? Take it from me, the wind shakes the tree-tops finely! He has many a time come whistling through my old branches; and how do you think that you'll come off, with that meagre display which you stick up in the air?"

"Every one grows in his own manner and we in ours," replied the young beeches. "This is the way it's done where we come from; and we dare say we are just as good as you."

"That's not a very polite remark to make to an old tree with moss on his branches," said the oak. "I am beginning to regret that I was so good to you. If you have a scrap of honour in your composition, then have the kindness to move your leaves a little to one side. Last year, there were hardly any buds on my lower branches, all through your standing in my light."

"We can't quite see what that has to do with us," replied the beeches. "Every one has enough to do to look after himself. If he is industrious and successful, then things go well with him. If not, he must be content to go to the wall. Such is the way of the world."

And the oak's lower branches died and he began to be terribly frightened.

"You're nice fellows, you are," he said, "the way you reward me for my hospitality! When you were little, I let you grow on my food and protected you against the storm. I let the sun shine on you whenever he wanted to and I treated you as if you were my own children. And now you choke me by way of thanks."

"Fudge!" said the beeches.

Then they blossomed and put forth fruit and, when the fruit was ripe, the wind shook their branches and spread it all around.

"You are active people, like myself," said the wind. "That's why I like you and will gladly give you a hand."

And the fox rolled at the foot of the beech and filled his coat with the prickly fruit and ran all over the country with it. The bear did the same and moreover laughed at the old oak while he lay and rested in the shadow of the beech. The wood-mouse was delighted with the new food which he got and thought that beech-nuts tasted much better than acorns.

New little beeches shot up round about and grew just as quickly as their parents and looked as green and happy as if they did not know what a bad conscience was.

But the old oak gazed out sadly over the forest. The light beech-leaves peeped forth on every hand and the oaks sighed and told one another their troubles.

"They are taking our power from us," they said and shook themselves as well as they could for the beeches. "The land is no longer ours."

One branch died after the other and the storm broke them off and flung them to the ground. The old oak had now only a few leaves left in his top.

"The end is at hand," he said, gravely.

But there were many more people in the land now than before and they hastened to cut down the oaks while there were still some left:

"Oak makes better timber than beech," they said.

"So at last we get a little appreciation," said the old oak. "But we shall have to pay for it with our lives."

Then he said to the beech-trees:

"What was I thinking of, when I helped you on in your youth? What an old fool I have been! We oak-trees used to be lords of the land and now, year after year, I have had to see my brothers all around succumb in the struggle against you. I myself am almost done for and not one of my acorns has shot up, thanks to your shadow. But, before I die, I should like to know what you call your behaviour."

"That's soon said, old friend!" replied the beeches. "We call it competition and it's no discovery of ours. It's that which rules the world."

"I don't know those foreign words of yours," said the oak. "*I* call it rank ingratitude."

Then he died.

THE WEEDS

1

IT was a fine and fruitful year.

Rain and sunshine came turn and turn about, in just the way that was best for the corn. No sooner did the farmer think that it was getting rather dry, than he could be quite sure that it would rain the next day. And, if he was of opinion that he had had rain enough, then the clouds parted at once, just as though it were the farmer that was in command.

The farmer, therefore, was in a good humour and did not complain, as otherwise he always did. Glad and rejoicing, he walked over the land with his two boys.

"It will be a splendid harvest this year," he said. "I shall get my barns full and make lots of money. Then Jens and Ole shall have a new pair of trousers apiece and I will take them with me to market."

"If you don't cut me soon, farmer, I shall be lying down flat," said the rye and bowed her heavy ears right down to the ground.

Now the farmer could not hear this, but was quite able to see what the rye was thinking of; and so he went home to fetch his sickle.

"It's a good thing to be in the service of men," said the rye. "I can be sure now that all my grains will be well taken care of. Most of them will go to the mill and that, certainly, is not very pleasant. But afterwards they will turn into beautiful fresh bread; and one must suffer something for honour's sake. What remains the farmer will keep and sow next year on his land."

2

Along the hedge and beside the ditch stood the weeds. Thistle and burdock, poppy and bell-flower and dandelion grew in thick clusters and all had their heads full of seed. For them too it had been a fruitful year, for the sun shines and the rain falls on the poor weeds just as much as on the rich corn.

"There's no one to cut us and cart us to the barn," said the dandelion and shook her head, but very carefully, lest the seed should fall out too soon. "What is to become of our children?"

"It gives me a headache to think of it," said the poppy. "Here I stand, with many hundreds of seeds in my head, and I have no idea where to dispose of them."

"Let's ask the rye's advice," said the burdock.

And then they asked the rye what they ought to do.

"It doesn't do to mix in other people's affairs when one's well off," said the rye. "There is only one piece of advice that I will give you: mind you don't fling your silly seed over my field, or you'll have me to deal with!"

Now this advice was of no use to the wild flowers and they stood all day pondering as to what they should do. When the sun went down, they closed their petals to go to sleep, but they dreamt all night of their seed and the next morning they had found a remedy.

The poppy was the first to wake.

She carefully opened some little shutters in the top of her head, so that the sun could shine right in upon the seeds. Next, she called to the morning-wind, who was running and playing along the hedge.

"Dear wind," she said, pleasantly. "Will you do me a service?"

"Why not?" said the wind. "I don't mind having something to do."

"It's a mere trifle," said the poppy. "I will only ask you to give a good shake to my stalk, so that my seeds can fly far away out of the shutters."

"Right you are," said the wind.

And away flew the seeds to every side. The stalk certainly snapped; but that the poppy did not bother about. For, when one has provided well for one's children, there's really nothing left to do in this world.

"Good-bye," said the wind and wanted to go on.

"Wait a bit," said the poppy. "Promise me first that you won't tell the others. Else they might have the same idea and then there would be less room for my seed."

"I shall be silent as the grave," said the wind and ran away.

"Pst! Pst!" said the bell-flower. "Have you a moment to do me a tiny little service?"

"All right," said the wind. "What is it?"

"Oh, I only wanted to ask you to shake me a little," said the bell-flower. "I have opened some of the shutters in my head and I should like to have my seed sent a good distance out into the world. But you must be sure not to tell the others, or they might think of doing the same thing."

"Lord preserve us!" said the wind and laughed. "I shall be mute as a fish."

And then he gave the flower a thorough good shaking and went on.

"Dear wind, dear wind!" cried the dandelion. "Where are you off to so fast?"

"Is there anything the matter with you too?" asked the wind.

"Not a bit," said the dandelion. "I only wanted a word with you."

"Then be quick about it," said the wind, "for I am thinking seriously of going down."

"You see," said the dandelion, "it's very difficult for us this year to get all our seed settled; and yet one would like to do the best one can for one's children. How the bell-flower and the poppy and the poor burdock will manage I do not know, upon my word. But the thistle and I have combined and have hit upon an expedient. You shall help us."

"That makes four in all," thought the wind and could not help laughing aloud.

"What are you laughing at?" asked the dandelion. "I saw you whispering with the bell-flower and the poppy just now; but, if you tell them a thing, then you will simply get nothing out of me."

"What do you take me for?" said the wind. "Mum's the word! What is it you want?"

"We've put out a nice little umbrella right up at the top of our seed. It's the sweetest little toy you can think of. If you only just blow on me, it will fly up in the air and fall down wherever you please. Will you?"

"Certainly," said the wind.

And, whoosh! he blew over the thistle and the dandelion and took all their seeds with him across the fields.

3

The burdock still stood pondering. She was thick-headed and that was why she took so long. But, in the evening, a hare jumped over the hedge.

"Hide me! Save me!" he cried. "Farmer's Trust is after me."

"Creep round behind the hedge," said the burdock; "then I'll hide you."

"You don't look to me as if you were cut out for the job," said the hare; "but beggars can't be choosers."

And then he hid behind the hedge.

"Now, in return, you might take some of my seeds to the fields with you," said the burdock and she broke off some of her many burs and scattered them over the hare.

Soon after, Trust came running along the hedge.

"Here's the dog!" whispered the burdock and, with a bound, the hare leapt the hedge into the rye.

"Have you seen the hare?" asked Trust. "I can see that I'm getting too old for hunting. One of my eyes is quite blind and my nose can no longer find the scent."

"I have seen him," replied the burdock, "and, if you will do me a service, I will show you where he is."

Trust agreed and the burdock stuck some of her burs on to his back and said:

"Would you just rub yourself against the stile here, inside the field? But that's not where you're to look for the hare, for I saw him run into the wood a little while ago."

Trust carried the burs to the field and ran off to the wood.

"So now I've got my seeds settled," said the burdock and laughed to herself contentedly. "But goodness knows how the thistle is going to manage and the dandelion and the bell-flower and the poppy!"

4

Next spring, already the rye stood quite high.

"We are well off, considering all things," said the rye-stalks. "Here we are in a great company that contains none but our own good family. And we don't hamper one another in the very least. It's really an excellent thing to be in the service of men."

But, one fine day, a number of little poppies and thistles and dandelions and burdocks and bell-flowers stuck their heads up above the ground in the midst of the luxuriant rye.

"What's the meaning of this now?" asked the rye. "How in the world did *you* get here?"

And the poppy looked at the bell-flower and asked:

"How did *you* get here?"

And the thistle looked at the burdock and asked:

"How on earth did *you* get here?"

They were all equally surprised and it was some time before they had done explaining. But the rye was the angriest and, when she had heard all about Trust and the hare and the wind, she was quite furious.

"Thank goodness that the farmer shot the hare in the autumn," said she. "And Trust, luckily, is dead too, the old scamp! So I have no further quarrel with *them*. But how dare the wind carry the seed of the weeds on to the farmer's land!"

"Softly, softly, you green rye!" said the wind, who had been lying behind the hedge and had heard all this. "I ask no one's leave, but do as I please; and now I shall compel you to bow before me."

Then he blew over the young rye, so that the thin stalks swayed to and fro.

"You see," he then said, "the farmer looks after his rye, for that's *his* business. But the rain and the sun and I: we interest ourselves in all of you alike, without distinction of persons. For us the poor weeds are quite as attractive as the rich corn."

Now the farmer came out to look at his rye and, when he saw the weeds that stood in the fields, he was vexed and scratched his head and began to scold in his turn.

"That's that dirty wind," he said to Jens and Ole, who stood beside him with their hands in the pockets of their new trousers.

But the wind dashed up and blew off the hats of all three of them and trundled them ever so far away. The farmer and his boys ran after them, but the wind was the quicker. At last, he rolled the hats out into the pond and the farmer and his boys had to stand ever so long and fish for them before they got them out.

THE WATER-LILY AND THE DRAGON-FLY

1

A LITTLE stream ran between trees and bushes. Along the banks stood tall, slender reeds and whispered to the wind. In the middle of the water floated the water-lily, with her white flower and her broad, green leaves.

Generally the water was very still, but when, as sometimes happened, the wind went for a trip over the surface of the stream, then the reeds rustled and the water-lilies dived right down under the water and the leaves flew up or to either side, so that the thick green stalks, which came all the way from the bottom, found it difficult to hold them tight.

All day long, a dragon-fly grub crept up and down the water-lily's stem.

"What a terrible bore it must be," said the grub, looking up at the flowers, "to be a water-lily!"

"You speak of things which you don't understand," replied the water-lily. "It is just the pleasantest thing in the world."

"Well, I can't understand that," said the grub. "I should always want to be tearing myself free and flying round like a great, splendid dragon-fly."

"Nonsense!" said the water-lily. "A fine pleasure that would be! No, to lie peacefully on the water and dream and to drink sunshine and now and again to rock upon the waves: there's some sense in that."

The grub reflected for a moment and then said:

"I have higher aspirations. If I could have my way, I should be a dragon-fly. I should skim over the water on great stiff wings, kiss the white flowers, rest for a second on your leaves and then fly on again."

"You are ambitious," said the water-lily, "and that is silly. Wise people know when they are well off. May I make so free as to ask you what you would propose to do to turn into a dragon-fly? You don't look as if you were made for one. In any case, you must see that you grow up prettier; you're very gray and ugly now."

"Yes, that's the pity of it," said the grub, a little disheartened. "I myself don't know how it is to happen; but I still hope that it will. That's why I crawl around here and eat all the little insects I can catch."

"Ah, so you think you can eat yourself into something big!" said the water-lily, mockingly. "That would be a pleasant way of improving one's condition."

"Yes, but I believe it's the right way for me!" cried the dragon-fly grub. "I shall eat and eat all day, till I grow stout and fat, and then, one fine morning, I hope my fat will change into wings with gold on them and all the rest that a real dragon-fly wants."

The water-lily shook her wise white head:

"Let those foolish thoughts be," she said, "and learn to be contented with your lot. You can now live in peace and quiet among my leaves and creep up and down my stalk as much as ever you like. You have plenty of food and no cares nor worries: what more can you want?"

"You have an inferior nature," answered the grub, "and therefore you have no sense of higher things. I want to become a dragon-fly!"

And then she crept down to the bottom to catch lots of little insects and eat herself fatter than ever.

The water-lily lay quietly on the water and reflected:

"I can't understand animals!" she said to herself. "They do nothing but dance about from morn till night, hunt and eat one another and know no moment's peace. We flowers are more sensible. We grow up calmly and placidly, side by side, drink sunshine and rain and take everything as it comes. And I am the luckiest of them all. How often have I not floated contentedly here on the water, while the other flowers were suffering from the drought on land! We flowers are by far the happier; but that is what those stupid animals fail to see."

2

When the sun set in the evening, the dragon-fly grub lay very still on the stalk with her legs drawn up under her. She had eaten a heap of insects and was so fat that she felt as though she would burst. And yet she was not glad: she pondered on what the water-lily had said and could not sleep all night for restless thinking. And all that reflecting made her head ache, for it was a labour to which she was not used. And she felt pains in her back too and in her chest. It was as though she were going to be pulled to pieces and die on the spot.

When morning began to break, she could bear it no longer:

"I don't know what it is," she cried in despair. "These pains hurt so that I can't think what is to become of me. Perhaps the water-lily is right and I shall never be more than a poor, wretched grub. But the thought of that is too terrible! I should so love to turn into a dragon-fly and fly about in the sun. Oh, my back, my back! I *must* be dying!"

Again she felt as if her back was bursting and she screamed for pain. At the same moment, the reeds on the bank began to rustle.

"That is the morning-wind," thought the grub. "At least, let me see the sun once more before I die."

And, with a great effort, she crawled to one of the leaves of the water-lily, stretched out her legs and prepared for death.

But, when the sun had risen and stood red and motionless in the east, suddenly there came an opening right in the middle of the grub's back, accompanied by a frightful itching. Oh, the pain of it, the anguish! It was a terrible feeling. Almost swooning, she closed her eyes, but the agony and the itching grew no less. And then, suddenly, she perceived that the pain was gone; and, when she opened her eyes, she was hovering through the air on stiff, glittering wings, a brilliant dragon-fly! Beneath her, on the leaf of the water-lily, lay the ugly gray covering which she had worn as a grub.

"Hurrah!" cried the new dragon-fly. "Now the wish of my heart is fulfilled."

And she flew through the air as swiftly as though she meant to fly to the end of the earth.

"The hussy has got her way after all!" thought the water-lily. "Now we shall see if she is more contented than before."

3

Two days later, the dragon-fly came flying up and settled on the flowers of the water-lily.

"Good-morning," said the water-lily. "So you've come at last. I was beginning to think that you had grown too grand to come and see your old friends."

"Good-morning," said the dragon-fly. "Where shall I lay my eggs?"

"Oh, you'll find a place somewhere," replied the flower. "Sit down first and tell me if you are happier now than when you were an ugly little grub crawling up and down my stalk."

"Where can I lay my eggs? Oh, wherever can I lay my eggs?" cried the dragon-fly and flew buzzing from leaf to leaf, laying one here and one there, and at last sat down, tired and exhausted, on a leaf.

"Well?" said the water-lily.

"Oh, I was much better off then," sighed the dragon-fly. "The sunshine is glorious and it is a great delight to fly over the water, but I never have time to enjoy it. I tell you, I'm awfully busy. In the old days, I had nothing to think of. And now I have to fly about all day long to lay these silly eggs. I haven't a moment to myself and have hardly time to eat."

"What did I tell you?" cried the water-lily, triumphantly. "Didn't I prophesy that your happiness would be no greater?"

"Good-bye," said the dragon-fly, with a sigh. "I have no time to listen to you: I must go and lay more eggs."

But, just as she was about to fly away, the starling came:

"I say, I say, what a dear little dragon-fly!" he said. "Just a nice little mouthful for my youngsters!"

And with a whizz! he snapped up the dragon-fly in his beak and flew away with her.

"There they go!" cried the water-lily, shaking her leaves with anger. "Those animals, those animals! What extraordinary creatures they are. I must say I prefer my own quiet life. I hurt nobody and no one injures me. I am so hap...."

She got no further, for a boat glided close past her.

"Oh, what a lovely water-lily!" said Ellen, who sat in the stern. "I must have it."

She bent over the side and tore the flower away. When she got home, she put it into a glass of water, where it stood for three days with a lot of other flowers.

"I don't know what to think," said the water-lily, on the fourth day. "I have not fared a whit better than that poor dragon-fly."

"The flowers are faded," said Ellen and threw them out of the window.

And the water-lily lay with her fair white petals on the dirty ground.

AUNT EIDER-DUCK

1

IT was winter.

The leaves were gone from the trees and the flowers from the hedge. The birds too were gone, that is to say the more important ones; they had all departed for the South.

But some, of course, had remained behind.

There was the everlasting sparrow, for instance, and the nimble little titmouse, besides the crow and the raven, who looked twice as black and hungry against the snow. There were also a few birds who preferred to take the rough with the smooth rather than travel so far afield.

Down on the beach there was more life than in summer.

There were the gulls who plunged about, in great flocks, wherever a hole had been made in the ice. And there were the wild-duck, who swam in the open water and quacked and dived and flew up whenever a shot was heard from the fishermen's guns.

"What a crowd!" said the sparrow.

"They come from the North," said the gull. "From Norway and the Faroe Islands, where it is a hundred times colder than here. As soon as there is the least bit of a change in the temperature, they fly back again. Do you know those two who are coming this way over the ice?"

"How should I know them?" said the sparrow. "I was born last summer and I only wish I were back in the nest!"

"They are eider-ducks," said the gull. "Look, there's one more coming."

So there was. And he was a very handsome bird. He had a green neck, a white throat and a white breast, with a pink sheen on it, and lovely yellow legs.

"That is the drake," said the gull. "The other two are females and not so smart, although they don't look bad either."

The three eider-ducks had now come so near that the sparrow and the gull could hear what they were talking about.

"Dear lady," said the drake, "I cannot understand why you stay on the ice. Do come to the open water and let us all enjoy ourselves."

"Every word that he says is a lie," said auntie. "But, lord, how charming it is!"

"It's terrible!" said the sparrow and the gull. "Such a dear young lady!"

"Fiddle!" said auntie. "We all have to go through it. My seven husbands all said the same and not one of them kept his promise. But they were charming, for all that. Only they had not such green necks as this one. He's splendid. I could fall in love with him myself."

"When do we start?" asked Miss Eider-Duck.

"To-morrow early, my darling, if the wind is fair," said her beau.

"I'll go with you," said auntie. "In the first place, it's more proper. And then it's so charming to see young people so happy."

They started the next morning.

It was not yet light when the birds began their passage. Thousands of eider-duck flew along in successive flocks, while thousands more came up from every side. The gull and the sparrow woke up when they heard the screaming and singing in the air.

"Fancy going north in weather like this!" said the sparrow, shivering. "Why, it's colder than ever!"

"There's spring in the air when one's in love," said the gull.

2

Day and night, the northward flight proceeded.

There were so many birds that they were quite bewildering to see and, as time passed and they neared their destination, their longing increased and they flew as though there were fire under their wings. The aunt never left the young couple and was as light and swift as they and as happy as if she herself were going to be married for the eighth time.

At last they reached the Faroes, which were their home.

They screamed and quacked for joy when they saw the rocks rise from the sea and their wings beat with renewed vigour, tired though they were by the long journey. They fell upon the cliffs as upon a prey and soon there was not a spot left but a happy bird sat in it and flapped her wings and screamed.

"Now I'll show you a good place for a nest," said auntie to the young pair, who sat exchanging loving looks. "Come with me to the other side of the rock."

They flew with her and reached the place where the man to whom the rock belonged had put little wooden boxes for the birds. There was just one empty one left and the bridegroom at once took possession.

"Here you will be able to sit on the eggs safely and comfortably, my darling," he said.

"Yes—and you too," she answered. "Don't you remember that you promised to help me with my work?"

"I should think I did!" said he and kissed her.

"Lord, how charming!" said auntie.

"And I don't want to live in that nasty box," said the young duck. "I was looking forward most awfully to collecting sea-weed and straw and heather, as you told me you used to with your former wife. And that's what I want to do also."

"Be easy, my dear little girl," he said. "Of course, we will line the box a bit, but let us be glad that there is something to start on. Remember that we have a long life before us, full of work and happiness, and don't let us begin by doing more than we shall be able to keep up."

"Lord, how he lies!" said auntie and cast up her eyes to the sky. "But how lovely it is to listen to!"

"What did you say?" asked the little duck.

"I was saying that your future husband has the loveliest green neck in all the Faroes," said auntie. "I should like to give it a little bite. But now I will leave you to your happiness."

Then she flew quacking over the rock and splashed into the water with the others. The two young people began to line their box with what they could find. Soon the wedding took place, with mirth and pomp, and thousands of other young eider-duck were married on the same day.

"Lord, how beautiful it is to be young!" said auntie, who was paying wedding-visits with a swarm of other old ladies.

3

And the young couple were comfortable and very happy. But, when she had laid her first egg in the nest, they had a tiff.

He wanted her to go for a little trip with him over the rock, while the egg lay in the nest, and she had no objection, but she did think that he might have shown rather more pleasure at the sight of that fine gray-green egg.

"I am saving up my emotions," he said, "as befits a man. Come along."

Then she said, however, that it was out of the question to leave the egg lying like that, with nothing over it. They must cover it with something. She plucked some fine down from under her wings and laid it on the egg. But when she asked him to do the same, he shook his head with decision.

"I am saving up my feathers," he said. "You will lay four more eggs and my turn will come when you've run out of down. I shall pluck myself bald if it's for the good of our children."

"Lord, how he's romancing!" said auntie, who was standing near and heard all they said. "He's just like my own husbands. They don't mean a word of it, but still it does an old heart good to hear them."

The young wife now accompanied her husband to the beach, where all was life and jollity.

Scores of husbands were there with their wives and all the old gentlemen and ladies who no longer had a nest. They dived and chatted and told funny stories. But the young wife mostly sat apart or talked to the other young wives, who also were in a rather solemn mood. And soon she declared that she must positively lay another egg.

"Come, dear," she said. "Come, let us go home. There's a new egg coming."

"What a misfortune!" said her husband, who was in the midst of a quadrille with a couple of young ducks of the summer before, who were not yet thinking of marriage.

But he went back with her to the nest and she laid her egg. She plucked some more down, while he addressed her in beautiful and touching phrases, and then they went out again, for he simply could not stay at home in the nest.

But they had not gone half-way when she felt another egg coming and told him so.

"You had better stay up there in the nest," he said, crossly. "This running to and fro does not amuse me and is bad for the children's health."

"Won't you stay with me?" she asked.

"I'll come and have a look at you as often as I can," he said.

"And that's the way you keep the promises you made me!" said she and burst into tears.

"My own darling little wife!" he said. "I can't help you the least little bit with the eggs. You've got to lay them and lay them you must. My work for our dear children and for yourself will begin when the eggs are all laid and you have started hatching them. And then, of course, when the little darlings come out, they will have to be fed and taught how to get on in the world. I am saving up my strength till that time comes, you see. And then I will sit on the eggs, while you go for a nice little trip and play about with the others down below."

"Did you ever hear the like?" said auntie. "How beautifully he talks! You've got a really nice husband."

And so the young wife went back to the nest alone and laid her third egg. Auntie flew down to the beach with the husband:

"I'll look after him, dear," she whispered; "trust me for that."

And then the fourth egg came and the fifth.

She had plucked all the feathers from her breast that she thought she could spare and placed them in a nice little, mouse-gray heap around the eggs. Then she sat upon them herself and brooded and brooded. At first, from time to time, she went to the edge of the cliff to look down at the beach, where her husband was with the other men and the ladies who had no eggs. But she did this less and less often. She took no food, grew thin and brooded and brooded. Her aunt called every day to have a chat with her.

4

One day, the husband came and sat down by the nest. He looked very spruce with his green neck and his bright eyes.

"Well, how are you getting on?" he asked.

"I despise you," she said. "Go away and never show your face to me again. You coaxed me with your fair promises and not one of them have you kept. I have had to pluck all the down I wanted from my own breast. I've been sitting here alone, day after day, while you've been amusing yourself with all those revellers on the beach. You haven't brought me a bite of food."

"Tush!" he said, scratching in the sand with his fine, yellow feet. "I shall be pleased to bring you a small mussel from time to time, if that gives you any satisfaction. But, for goodness' sake, don't be so formal! Do you really imagine that men weigh their words when they're engaged?"

"Get out of this!" she screamed. "I don't want my children to see their unnatural father."

"Oh, as for that, I wouldn't give a straw to see that callow brood," he replied. "And, upon my word, you're no beauty yourself! You're so lean and full of bald spots. You're very different from the pretty girl I fell in love with."

She was about to fly up out of the nest and give him one for himself; but she lay as though rooted to the floor and stared at a man who put his head over the edge of the cliff. Her husband flew away with a loud scream and auntie did the same. But the man hardly gave them a glance. He scrambled up the rock and set down a great basket, which he carried, beside the nest.

"What a fine nest!" he said. "There's down enough here to stuff a little pillow with."

"What do you want?" asked the eider-duck.

"I shan't hurt you," said the man. "It would be silly of me to do you any harm; why, I put the box here for you myself. I only want the down that's in your nest."

"Never!" cried the bird, spreading out her wings and holding on to the nest as fast as she could. "What should I do with my children?"

"Why, pluck some more down from your pretty breast, my dear," said the man, kindly. "Now stand aside and let me get by, without any nonsense. After all, I'm the stronger of the two and the nest belongs to me."

But the young eider-duck did not stir from her place. She pecked at his hands with her beak and cried:

"Go down to the beach and catch my husband and my old aunt! Kill them, if you like, and take all their down. It's only what they deserve. But you must let my down be!"

"Stuff, my pet!" said the man. "The best down is what a mother plucks from her breast. We all know that. And, if your children have to do without, it will come in useful for other children, dainty little human children, whose parents can afford to buy the softest little pillows for them."

"At least, wait until my children are ready!" cried the eider-duck in despair.

"A nice thing!" said the man. "What, let you lie there and spoil the down? Come, clear out!"

He pushed her aside, took all the down, put it in his basket and went away, saying:

"Pluck some more feathers if you want them for your young. That's what a good mother always does."

Then she went to the edge of the rock and looked out.

The eider-duck were disporting themselves gloriously. She could distinctly see her husband and her aunt diving and amusing themselves as though life were a sheer enjoyment. And all the others were doing the same: not one of them thought that there was a man up above emptying all the nests of their precious down.

"Come up here and pluck your breast!" she screamed. "Now is the time to keep some of your promises. Your eggs are lying bare and cold, while you are enjoying yourself down there, you wretch!"

But her voice died away in the noise of the wind and surf. No one heard her cries or beheld her despair. She remembered that the eggs were really getting cold, while she stood there, and she hurried back to the nest.

One of the eggs began to burst and soon a tiny beak peeped out of the hole in the shell. She now flew to help the little chap out. She stood gazing at him for a moment and saw what a darling he was. And then, like a mad thing, she began to pluck the last remaining feathers from her breast and every part of her and laid them round the little fellow. She ceased complaining and thought only of how she could make her children warm and comfortable.

5

Two days later, all the five young ones were out.

The young mother saw with pride how smart they were. Already, they stretched out their feet, which had a delicate web between the toes, yawned, lifted their little wings and even quacked a bit.

"You must go to the beach at once," she said. "I am sure that there are no prettier children on the whole rock. But, should you meet your wretch of a father, mind you look the other way."

She went down the rock and the five little ones followed so nimbly that it was a joy to see. Half-way down, she met her aunt:

"I was just coming up to see you," said the old lady. "I say, what darlings your five children are!"

"Aren't they dears?" said the mother, who forgot all her rage when she heard her aunt's praises.

"Let me take one of them to walk with," said auntie.

"Not while I live!" said the mother, severely. "I know too well how flighty you are, auntie. My children are mine and nobody else's and mine they shall remain."

At that moment, a shot rang out through the air.

It was a silly shot, fired at random by a silly boy who wanted to show off his father's gun. But the gun was loaded and the shot spread and Mother Eider-Duck sank to the ground with a scream.

"My young ones! My young ones!" she moaned.

"They're all right, all five of them," said auntie. "Be easy. But what's the matter?"

"I'm dying," said the mother. "I am full of shot. I know for certain that I'm dying. Oh, my children, my children!"

"Never mind about them," said auntie. "I shall be a mother to them in your stead and look after them as if they were my own."

"Oh, auntie," said the mother, in a feeble voice, "you are so terribly frivolous. I have seen you myself from up there, playing and fooling about with the men and the girls on the beach. How can a mother trust her children to you?"

"What do you mean?" asked auntie. "Surely, it's quite different when one has children to care for. You just die in peace, do you hear?"

And that is what Mother Eider-Duck did.

She sank into herself and only just had time to take a last look at her children. But her aunt did not even wait till she was quite dead. She forgot everything, except that she had suddenly got five beautiful children, and at once walked off with them to the beach. She knew the nearest way, because she had already been there several times with children. She made the road easy for them and helped them in every possible manner, fondling them with her beak and praising or scolding them according to their deserts.

By the time that their mother had closed her eyes, the children were down on the beach.

They at once swam and dived in a way that was a joy to see. Auntie watched over them and almost burst with pride. An old beau came up and asked her to take a walk with him, but she gave him a smart rap with her beak:

"Don't you see the children, you old coxcomb?" she said. "Get out of this, or I'll teach you!"

And she remained with the children until they were able to take care of themselves. She travelled to the South with them, winter after winter, and listened to the men courting them and befooling them, just as their father had done to their mother. She showed them good places for their nests, paid wedding-visits and was honoured and esteemed all over the rock, until, one day, a sea-eagle came and caught her and gobbled her up.

THE END

FOOTNOTES:

[1] Danish: *Edderkop*.

Milton Keynes UK
Ingram Content Group UK Ltd.
UKHW050650260624
444769UK00004B/188